Basic Knitting
And Projects

Leigh Ann Chow, editor

Anita J. Tosten and Missy Burns,
knitters and consultants

Photographs by Alan Wycheck
and Cyndi Klose

Illustrations by Marjorie Leggitt
and David Bienkowski

STACKPOLE
BOOKS

0 11557 01353 5

Copyright © 2014 by Stackpole Books

Published by
STACKPOLE BOOKS
5067 Ritter Road
Mechanicsburg, PA 17055
www.stackpolebooks.com

Printed in U.S.A.

10 9 8 7 6 5 4 3 2 1
First edition

Cover design by Wendy Reynolds

Photographs by Alan Wycheck except where otherwise noted.
Illustrations on pages 13, 16, 17, 21, 22, 24, 25, 30, 31, 32, 33, 35, 36, 37, 38, 39, 40, 41, 42, 43, 46, 49, 50, 53, 54, 69, 71, 72, 73, 74, 93, and 108 by Marjorie Leggitt.
Illustrations on pages 82, 83, 86, 87, and 99 by David Bienkowski.
Photo on page 130 (bottom) and illustrations on page 131 by Fleurtje Eliza.
Photos on pages 113, 114, 115, 122, 123, 124, 125, 127, 128, 129, 130 (top), 132, 146, 149, 150, 152, 156, 157, 158, 160, 162, 163, 164, 167, 171, 172, and 173 by Cyndi Klose.
Photos on pages 27, 28, 89, 90, and 91 by Mark Allison.

Gillian Cowl and Adirondack Mittens designed and © by Kathryn Fulton.
McDaisy Tablet or Laptop Sleeve designed and © by Fleurtje Eliza.
Universal Kite Shawlette designed and © by Tanja Fleischer.
Roxbury Park Cardigan designed and © by Brenda Castiel.
Bottom-Up Cardigan designed and © by Erika Flory.
Wintry Mix Hat designed and © by Andrea Sanchez.
All other patterns designed and © by Anita J. Tosten.

The twice-worked bind-off used in Lantz Corners Shawl (page 174) is the creation of Judy Pascale.

The first 30 rounds of the Lantz Corners Shawl are taken from James Norbury's *Traditional Knitting Patterns from Scandinavia, the British Isles, France, Italy and other European Countries* (Dover Publications, 1973).

Library of Congress Cataloging-in-Publication Data

Basic knitting and projects / Leigh Ann Chow, editor ; Anita J. Tosten and Missy Burns, knitters and consultants ; photographs by Alan Wycheck ; illustrations by Marjorie Leggitt and David Bienkowski. — First edition.
      pages cm
   Includes index.
   ISBN 978-0-8117-1353-5
   1. Knitting—Patterns.   I. Chow, Leigh Ann, editor of compilation.
TT825.B36   2014
746.43'2—dc23
                                                                    2013041590

Contents

Introduction

Knitting is a craft that is presently enjoying a renaissance of sorts. Around the world, people young and old are discovering—or rediscovering—the joy of working with needles and yarn. First practiced in ancient times, hand knitting has evolved from a necessary means of producing socks and stockings into a craft that is limited only by a knitter's creativity.

This book is intended to serve as a comprehensive introduction to the basic skills you will need to master in order to become a knitter. The focus of the first half of the book is on detailed, step-by-step text and photo sequences that will teach you how to execute the basic stitches and techniques of knitting. The second half of the book consists of projects that will allow you to use these skills to create beautiful handmade garments and accessories. We recommend that you spend your first hours with this book in the Basics section, learning and mastering the fundamental stitches and techniques. Then, once you are comfortable working with needles and yarn, you can move on to the projects—perhaps starting with one of the eaiser ones at the beginning of that section, then moving on to the more difficult ones. Check the skills box at the beginning of each pattern to see what skills are needed to make it (as well as where to find the instructions for each skill).

Pick up your needles and yarn and get ready to learn how to knit!

PART I

Skills

CHAPTER 1

The Basics

Tools and Materials

Yarn

Color

Yarn comes in as many colors as the rainbow: reds, oranges, yellows, greens, blues, indigos, violets, and every shade in between. Variegated yarns combine several complementary colors into one multihued skein.

Most yarn is dyed commercially in batches, or lots. The color of these batches can vary from one to another and the differences in color will become obvious when switching from one skein to another in a knitted garment. To avoid any potential color discrepancies, make sure to purchase enough yarn to complete your project all at once, making sure to check the skeins' labels to ensure that the dye lot number is the same.

Your local yarn shop will offer yarn in as many colors, weights, and textures as you can imagine.

Weight

Yarn also comes in a range of different weights. From the super fine yarn that is perfect for knitting soft, delicate baby blankets up to the super bulky wool used to knit thick, heavy sweaters, a yarn's weight has a great impact on the finished knitted product. Typically, when you knit a project from a pattern, it will specify the type of yarn to be used. In order to complete the project as the designer intended, it is important to conform to the suggested yarn weight or, if making a substitution, to come as close as possible to the recommended knit gauge. If, however, you are designing your own garment, a knowledge of the various yarn weights will help you to select a yarn that is most appropriate to the finished garment you are preparing to knit.

In order to provide a measure of consistency in yarn labeling, the Craft Yarn Council of America (CYCA) issued a set of standards for describing yarn weight. The guidelines organized yarn into 6 main weight categories, ranging from Super Fine (1) up to Super Bulky (6). In between are Fine (2), Light (3), Medium (4), and Bulky (5). Later, another yarn weight category was added, Lace (0). See the appendix on page 184 for more details on this organizational structure.

The CYCA's 6 main yarn weight categories (from top to bottom): Super Fine, Fine, Light, Medium, Bulky, and Super Bulky.

Composition and Structure

The vast majority of knitting yarn is created by spinning fibers together. Fibers can be natural, such as wool, mohair, silk, or cotton; man-made, such as acrylic, nylon, or polyester; or a blend of the two. Each fiber has its own distinctive characteristics and properties, some of which are desirable and others which are less so. Wool, for example, is extremely warm, but is not as strong as other fibers. Acrylic, on the other hand, is extremely durable but does not breathe well. Sometimes a blend of the two materials maximizes the advantages of each. For example, a sock yarn made of a 92% wool and 8% acrylic blend combines the warmth and comfort of natural wool with the added strength and resilience of synthetic fiber.

Z and S Twist

A yarn with a Z twist (left) has twists turning upward and to the right while an S twist (right) has twists turning upward and to the left.

The way in which the yarn's fibers are spun together determines its structure. There are a variety of different yarn structures:

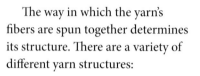

Spiral: A thinner yarn twisted around a thicker yarn.

Chenille: A velvety pile, wrapped with two thin, twisted threads. Can be either long-pile or short-pile.

Boucle: Two strands twisted at varying tensions, held together with a thin binding thread to produce loops of yarn.

Nubby: Two strands twisted so that one overlaps another to produce a bumpy texture.

Slubby: A strand that is alternately thick and thin, twisted with either a smooth or a slubby second strand.

Tape: Yarn made of knitted threads and woven into a narrow, flat band.

Novelty Yarns: Most common types combine metallic threads or feature long "eyelash" textures.

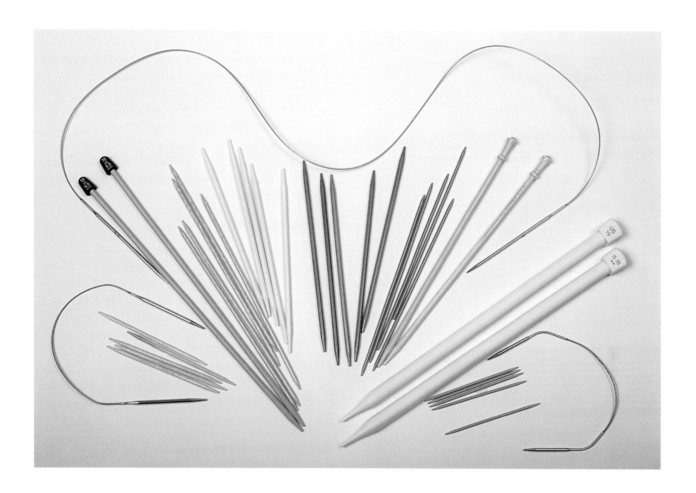

Knitting Needles

Aside from yarn, the knitting needle is the knitter's fundamental tool. Needles come in three main varieties: straight, circular, or double pointed. They range in both length and size from a 2.25 mm size 1 needle up to a 25 mm size 50 needle.

Needles come in a range of different materials: aluminum, steel, plastic, bamboo, or wood. The last two materials are typically more expensive but can be more pleasurable to knit with.

Small Needle Sizes

Knitting needle sizes are almost—but not quite—standardized. While the sizes for the larger needles are mostly standard, there is some variation in the smaller sizes. You can get size 1 needles in 2.25 mm or 2.5 mm; size 2 needles, likewise, maybe measuring 2.75 mm or 3 mm. When purchasing or selecting needles, pay attention to the size in millimeters for more accurate results.

Knitting Needle Sizes*

Millimeter Range	U.S. Size Range
2.25 mm	1
2.75 mm	2
3.25 mm	3
3.5 mm	4
3.75 mm	5
4 mm	6
4.5 mm	7
5 mm	8
5.5 mm	9
6 mm	10
6.5 mm	10½
8 mm	11
9 mm	13
10 mm	15
12.75 mm	17
15 mm	19
19 mm	35
25 mm	50

* From the Craft Yarn Council's standards for knitting needle sizes.

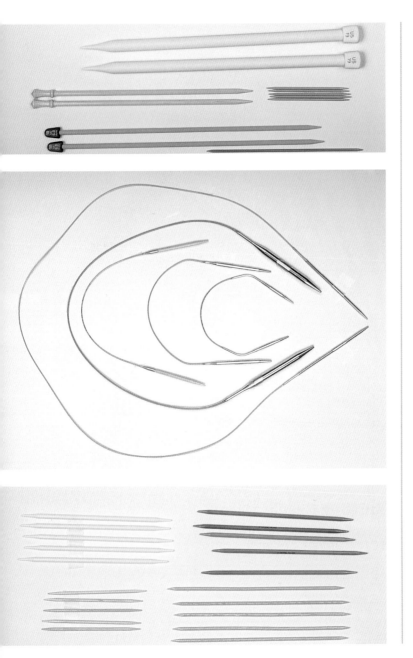

Straight Needles

Most knitters start off using straight needles; they are the simplest and most straightforward tool a knitter has to get the job done. Typically, straight needles are used to knit back and forth across a flat piece of knitting. Straight needles come in lengths ranging from 8 to 16 inches. Most small beginning projects such as scarves or children's garments are best completed on 10-inch needles, but larger projects such as adult sweaters require a 16-inch needle to accommodate all the stitches.

Circular Needles

Circular needles are typically used when knitting in the round. Knitting on circular needles produces a seamless, tubular piece of knitting, perfect when creating a hat or the body of a sweater. Circular needles come in various sizes: 12, 16, 20, 24, 32, and 40-inch lengths are available. Always use the length of needle that your pattern indicates. Knitting on a longer needle than is indicated will stretch the stitches and distort the final piece. Circular needles can also be used in place of straight needles to do flat knitting by simply turning the work from right to wrong side rather than knitting in the round (see box below).

Double-Pointed Needles

Double-pointed needles are generally used when working small projects in the round, such as socks, mittens, or gloves. When using double-pointed needles, the stitches are divided evenly over three, or sometimes four, needles, and the remaining needle is used to work the stitches. The resulting seamless garment is the same as that produced by the circular needle, but a set of double-pointed needles allows you to easily maneuver around the knitted piece within a tighter radius. Double-pointed needles usually come in sets of 4 or 5 needles and in lengths of 7 or 10 inches.

Straight vs. Circular Needles

While straight needles are more basic and less expensive than circular needles, circular needles do offer some advantages that make them worth considering. The main benefit of using a circular needle over a pair of straight needles is basically one of comfort: knitting in a small space (such as on an airplane or in a car) is much easier with circular needles than with straight needles, which protrude outward from the knitting. Circular needles also allow the bulk of the stitches to slide around onto the plastic tubing that connects the two needles. This allows you to rest the work in your lap while knitting the stitches remaining on the needles rather than having to hold all of the stitches up on the right needle as you complete those on the left. Before you purchase needles for your first project, think about where you will be knitting and how important comfort is to you. It might just be worth spending the few extra dollars to purchase the circular needles.

Other Tools

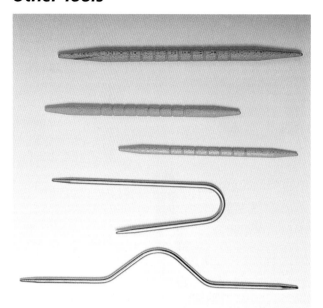

Cable Needles

Used to hold stitches when working cables (see page 76).

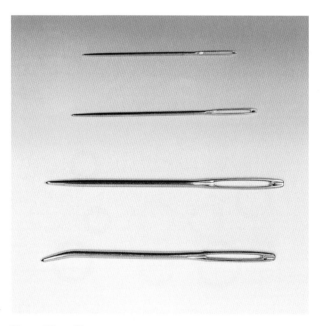

Yarn Needles

Also known as tapestry needles, these large, blunt sewing needles are used in finishing to sew up seams and weave in ends (see page 59). They come in both straight and bent-tipped varieties.

Tape Measure

Used to measure knitted pieces or people to determine the fit of a garment. Can also be used to check gauge.

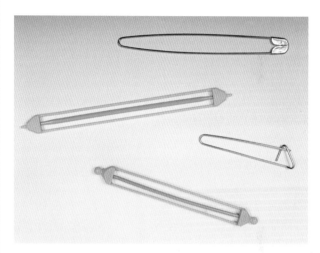

Stitch Holders

Used to temporarily hold a group of stitches while continuing to knit others. You can also use a piece of scrap yarn as a stitch holder.

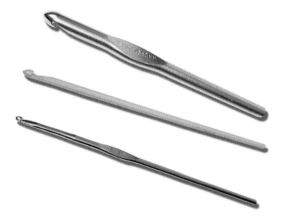

Crochet Hooks

Used to correct mistakes by rescuing dropped stitches (see page 48) or to create trims and accents in finishing.

Point Protectors

Used to cap the tip of the needle to prevent stitches from slipping off the ends when you're not knitting. They come in a variety of shapes and sizes.

Seaming Pins

Used to hold knitted pieces together when sewing seams or when blocking a large garment (see page 55).

Small Scissors or Yarn Cutter

Used to cut yarn. The pendant pictured here contains a recessed blade accessible through the notches in its edges.

Stitch Markers

Slipped over a needle to indicate start of a round of circular knitting (see page 92). Split markers can be used to indicate placement of seams or stitches.

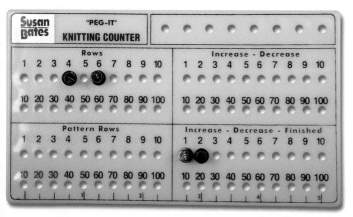

Row Counters

Used to keep track of rows as you knit. The round ones slip over a single-pointed needle for easy access. The pegboard keeps track of both rows and increases and decreases in more complicated patterns.

Coilless Pins

Used like a split ring marker to indicate placement. Regular safety pins' coils get caught in yarn.

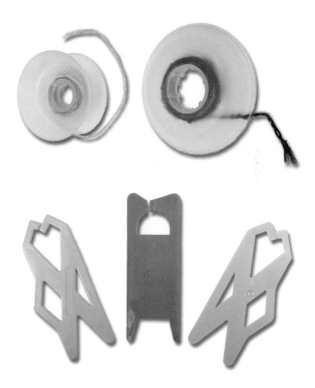

Bobbins

Used to hold small portions of yarn when knitting individual rows with more than one color or when doing intarsia knitting.

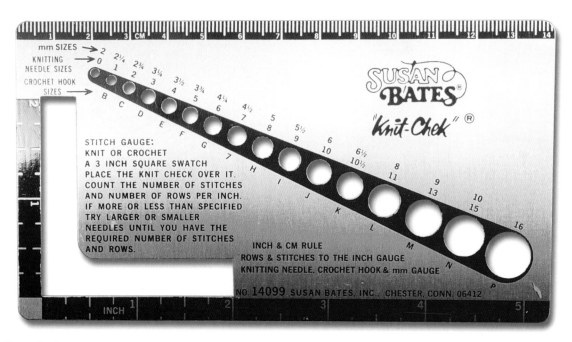

Needle/Stitch Gauge

Used to check gauge of knitted swatch (see page 64) as well as to confirm size of unknown knitting needles.

Ball Winder/Yarn Swift

Used to wind hanks of yarn into easy-to-use balls. Both clamp onto the edge of a table or countertop.

Making a Slip Knot

The first step in beginning to knit is creating a slip knot.

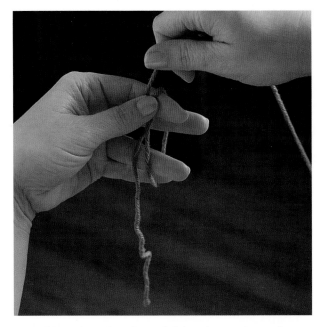

1. Holding the palm of your left hand toward you, drape 8 inches of yarn over the four fingers of your left hand, leaving a 5-inch tail. Wrap the yarn around the back of your fingers and back around to the front, stopping at your index finger. Hold down the end of the yarn with your thumb.

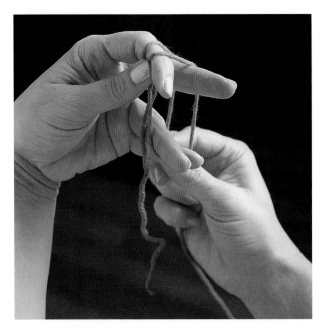

2. Continue the wrap around the back of your hand, stopping when you reach your little finger.

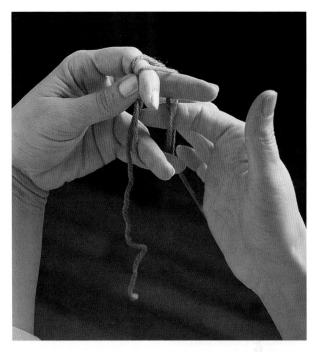

3. Spread your index and middle fingers slightly, and pull the working yarn up and through the loop.

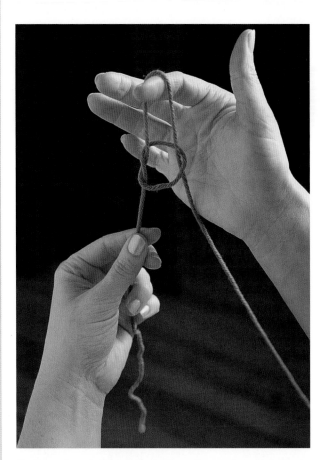

4. Once the working yarn is through, gently pull the loop off your fingers while holding onto the tail end of the yarn to form the knot.

5. Slide the loop onto the needle and pull the working yarn to tighten the loop on the needle.

A finished slip knot on the needle

Casting On

Casting on creates the stitches with which you will begin to knit. There are two basic methods of casting on: the cable and the long-tail.

Cable Cast-On

This simple, versatile cast-on is best suited for knitted pieces with non-elastic edges, such as scarves and afghans, that do not include ribbing.

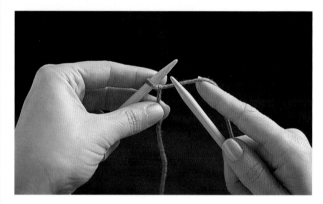

1. Hold the needle that has the slip knot in your left hand, supporting the needle between your thumb and middle finger. Grasp the loose end of the yarn between the tips of your middle finger and thumb. Hold the yarn and right needle as explained on pages 18–20.

2. Insert the tip of the right needle into the loop beneath the left needle, from right to left.

> **TIP»** If you properly support the left needle between your middle finger and thumb, your index finger will be free to help manipulate the yarn.

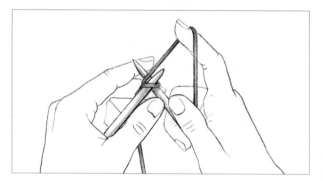

3. Holding the working yarn in your right hand, wrap the yarn counterclockwise (around) the tip of the right needle.

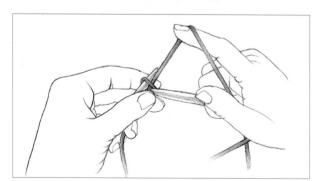

4. Using your right index finger (or left index finger for Continental knitters—see page 19 for an explanation of Continental and English knitting) for tension, pull the yarn down and through the loop with the tip of the right needle.

A newly created loop on your right needle

5. Transfer the new loop on your right needle back onto your left needle and pull the working yarn gently to tighten.

6. Repeat Steps 2–5, using the newly made loop on the left needle each time, until you have cast on the required number of stitches.

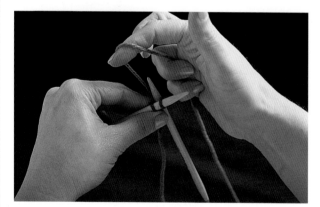

Repeating Step 2

Repeating Step 4

Repeating Step 5

A full row of cast-on stitches

TIP» Don't pull your cast-on stitches too tight on the needle. They should be loose enough that the needle slips comfortably beneath each new loop.

Long-Tail Cast-On

For garments such as sweaters, socks, or hats that require a more elastic edge, the long-tail cast-on is a better choice than the cable method. In this method, you estimate how much yarn will be required for the cast-on stitches, leaving enough yarn for an adequate tail.

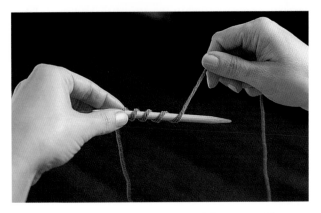

1. Estimate how much yarn you need for your tail by simply wrapping the yarn around the needle, one wrap for each stitch to be cast on. Add an additional 3-inch length of yarn to weave in later.

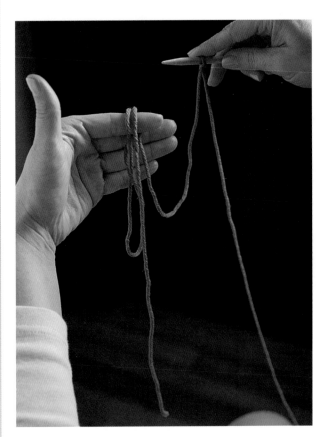

2. Unwrap the loops and use that length as the tail. Make a slip knot as explained on pages 11–12.

3. Holding the needle with the loop on it in your right hand, let the working yarn and tail hang straight down from the needle, with the working yarn behind the tail. Hold the thumb and index finger of your left hand together.

4. Insert your thumb and index finger in between the two dangling pieces of yarn.

5. Pull the needle toward you, wrapping the working yarn clockwise around your left index finger and the tail counterclockwise around your thumb. (This process looks a lot like making a slingshot.)

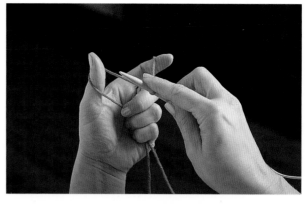

6. Draw both ends into your palm and hold them down with your remaining fingers. The needle in your right hand and your left hand with the yarn should be straight up and down, with a little slack between the two.

7. Push the needle up through the loop on your thumb from the bottom.

8. Catch the working yarn on your index finger and draw it down through the loop.

9. Pull the working yarn through the loop.

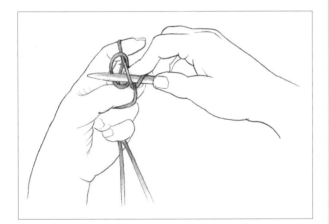

10. Release the loop of yarn from your thumb, gently pulling down on the tail with your thumb to tighten the loop.

11. Continue pulling down with your thumb until the loop is snug on the needle.

12. Reposition the yarn on your thumb and index finger and repeat Steps 6–11 until you have the required number of stitches.

Repeating Step 6

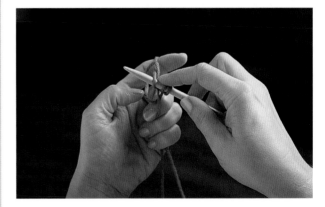

Repeating Step 10

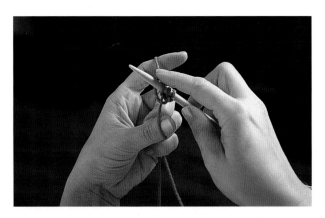

Repeating Step 11

TIP» Don't let go of the yarn in your palm. Make sure when you re-wrap the yarn around your thumb that you wrap counterclockwise.

Stitches cast on by the long-tail method

TIP» This method produces a cast-on that is smooth on the front and bumpy on the back. Because of this, the first row of your knitting must be a wrong-side row (for example, if you are knitting in stockinette stitch, start with a purl row rather than a knit row).

The Long-Tail Cast-On

If you think of the pieces of yarn on your fingers as individual strands, numbered from front to back, you will pass the needle under 1 and over 2, over 3, and then pull 3 back through 1 and 2. (You never touch 4.)

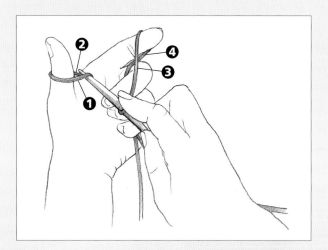

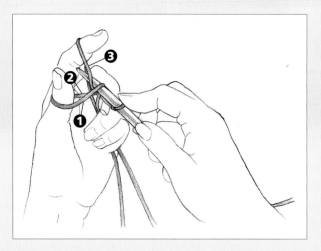

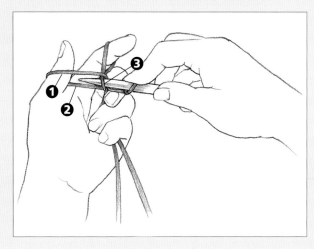

Holding Yarn and Needles

Once you have a row of cast-on stitches, you are ready to explore the two methods of holding the yarn and needles: the English method and the Continental method. Work through the general explanations of each method to see which you prefer.

At first it may feel awkward to hold the yarn and needles as shown, but over time that clumsy feeling diminishes as you gain more control. The initial goal of a beginning knitter is to hold the yarn and needles in such a way that it allows the knitter to obtain an even and consistent gauge (see page 64 for more about gauge). To begin, use a shorter pair of needles in a medium size—a 6, 7, or 8 will work well.

Hold the needles loosely, like this.

Left-Handed Knitters

Unlike many crafts, knitting is primarily an ambidextrous activity. Other than using the tapestry needle to bind off or sew up seams and the scissors to snip the yarn, the left-handed knitter should be able to learn how to knit in exactly the same manner as the right-handed knitter. It may be easier, however, for lefties to learn using the Continental method.

English vs. Continental Knitting Methods

Although the majority of knitters in North America and Great Britain knit by holding the working yarn in their right hand (known as the English method), in Germany, France, and most other European countries, knitters hold the working yarn in their left hand (known as the Continental method). English-style knitters "throw" the yarn over the needle, while Continental-style knitters "pick" the yarn through the loop. Both methods produce the same basic end product, so the choice of method is a personal one that depends mainly on how you were first taught to knit. Some knitters prefer the Continental style, as it is faster and more efficient than the English style. The best advice for beginners who have not yet developed a preference is to try both methods and stick with whichever one feels more comfortable. If you do choose to knit Continental-style, however, it is essential to form the stitches exactly as described on pages 22–23 and 25–26 in order to avoid twisting them.

English-style knitting

Continental-style knitting

English Method

1. Hold both needles in your left hand by crossing the right needle tip under the left needle tip and grasping both between your thumb and middle finger. Drape the yarn attached to the ball (referred to as the working yarn) over the little finger of your right hand.

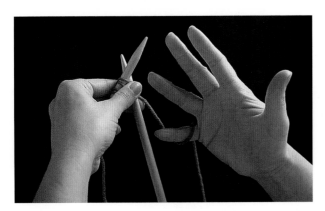

2. Wrap the yarn clockwise around your little finger for tension.

3. Insert your index finger under the working yarn between your little finger and the needle. You will use your index finger to carry the yarn around the tip of the right needle. With the index finger still holding the yarn, pass the right needle (on the bottom) into your right hand.

Continental Method

1. Hold the needle with the cast-on stitches in your right hand, with the working yarn draped over the little finger of your left hand.

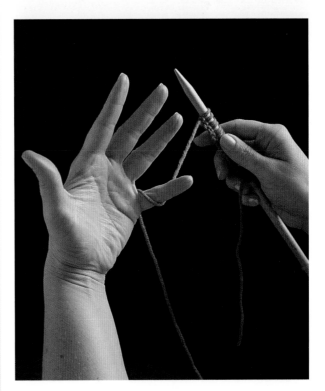

2. Wrap the yarn counterclockwise around your finger for tension.

3. Wrap the yarn over the index finger of your left hand, leaving about 2 inches of yarn between your index finger and the needle.

4. Return the needle with the cast-on stitches to your left hand, supporting the needle with your thumb and middle and ring fingers.

NOTE » Throughout this book, the majority of examples are illustrated by an English-style knitter. In most cases, knitting method has no impact on the technique involved in forming a stitch. Where there are significant differences between the two methods (as in the yarn over on page 71), both methods will be shown.

Knit

There are two basic stitches used in knitting: knit and purl. Both the English and Continental methods of knitting are shown here. To learn how to knit, first cast on 20 stitches using the cable method discussed on pages 12–14.

Knit Stitch: English Method

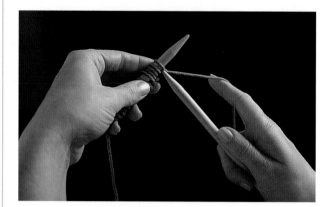

1. Hold the needle with the cast-on stitches in your left hand. Push the top stitch down about 1 inch from the tip of the needle.

2. Wrap the working yarn around your right index finger and hold it with the empty right needle in your right hand (as shown on page 18). Insert the tip of the right needle into the first stitch on the left needle from front to back, under the left needle.

Yarn pulled through stitch

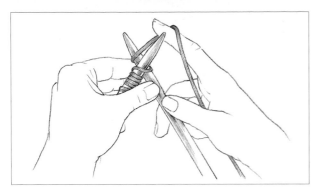

3. Using your right index finger, pass the yarn counterclockwise around the right needle and hold it there, parallel to the first stitch. Keep the tension comfortably tight with your right index finger.

5. Slip the first stitch off the left needle, leaving the newly knit stitch on the right one. You have just knit one stitch.

6. Repeat Steps 2–5 to knit through all the stitches on the left needle. You should always have a total of 20 stitches between the two needles. As you progress through the row, keep sliding the stitches on the right needle down to prevent them from bunching up. Keep your knitting loose enough that the stitches slide easily along the needle.

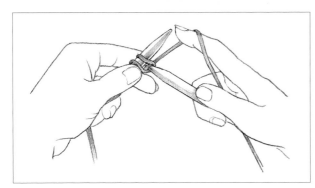

4. Use the tip of the right needle to pull the yarn down and through the stitch on the left needle.

7. When you have transferred all the stitches on your left needle to the right, you have completed one row of knitting. Turn the work around, making the old right needle the new left one, and vice versa, and knit a few more rows for practice. Knitting every row forms a pattern known as garter stitch, the most basic pattern. The resulting swatch will look the same on both sides.

Knit Stitch: Continental Method

1. Wrap the working yarn around your left hand and hold it with the needle with the cast-on stitches as shown on page 18. Push the top stitch down about 1 inch from the tip of the needle.

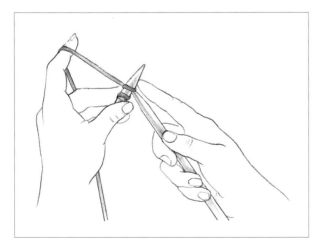

2. Insert the empty right needle into the first stitch on the left needle from front to back, under the left needle.

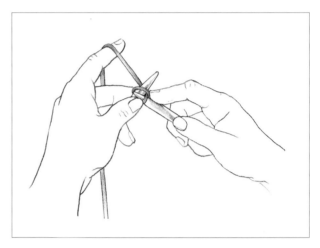

3. Catch the working yarn by putting the tip of the right needle on top of and behind it. Use your middle finger to help guide the yarn over the tip of the right needle. Pull the yarn through the stitch on the left needle.

4. Slip the first stitch off the left needle, leaving the newly knit stitch on the right one. You have just knit one stitch.

5. Repeat Steps 2–4 to knit through all the stitches on the left needle. You should always have a total of 20 stitches between the two needles. As you progress through the row, keep sliding the stitches on the right needle down to prevent them from bunching up. Keep your knitting loose enough that the stitches slide easily along the needle.

6. When you have transferred all the stitches on your left needle to the right, you have completed one row of knitting. Turn the work around, making the old right needle the new left one, and vice versa, and knit a few more rows for practice. Knitting every row forms a pattern known as garter stitch, the most basic pattern. The resulting swatch will look the same on both sides.

Purl

The purl stitch is the opposite of the knit stitch. Both the English and Continental methods of purling are shown here. To learn how to purl, first cast on 20 stitches using the cable method discussed on pages 12–14.

Purl Stitch: English Method

1. Hold the needle with the stitches in your left hand. Push the top stitch down about 1 inch from the tip of the needle.

2. Holding the working yarn in front of the needle, insert the tip of the right needle into the first stitch on the left needle from back to front, in front of the left needle. Hold both needles between the thumb and index finger of your left hand.

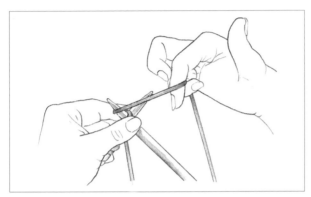

3. Using your right index finger, pass the yarn counter-clockwise around the right needle.

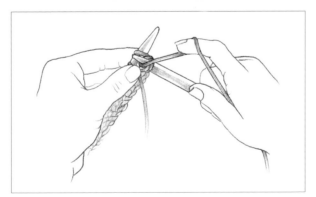

4. Use the tip of the right needle to pull the yarn back and through the stitch on the left needle.

5. Continue pulling the yarn completely through the stitch.

6. Slip the first stitch off the left needle, leaving the newly purled stitch on the right one. You have just purled one stitch.

7. Repeat Steps 2–6 to purl through all the stitches on the left needle. You should always have a total of 20 stitches between the two needles. As you progress through the row, keep sliding the stitches on the right needle down to prevent them from bunching up. Keep your knitting loose enough that the stitches slide easily along the needle.

8. When you have transferred all the stitches on your left needle to the right, you have completed one row of purling. Turn the work around, making the old right needle the new left one, and vice versa, and purl a few more rows for practice.

> **TIP»** When doing the first purl stitch of the row, it is important to insert the right needle into the stitch on the left needle before wrapping the yarn around your finger. This ensures that the yarn is in the right position before beginning your stitch. This only applies to the first stitch in the row; in subsequent stitches the yarn is already in the correct position.

Purl Stitch: Continental Method

1. Wrap the working yarn around your left hand and hold it with the needle containing the cast-on stitches as shown on page 18. Push the top stitch down about 1 inch from the tip of the needle.

2. Holding the working yarn in front of the left needle, insert the empty right needle into the first stitch on the left needle from back to front, in front of the left needle.

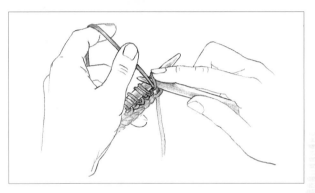

3. Using your left thumb to guide it, place the yarn over the tip of the right needle from front to back, parallel to the stitch on the left needle.

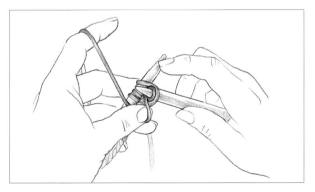

4. Using your thumb to keep tension on the working yarn, pull the loop up and through the stitch on the left needle.

5. Pull the loop the rest of the way through the first stitch and slip it off the left needle, leaving the newly purled stitch on the right one. You have just purled one stitch.

6. Repeat Steps 2–5 to purl through all the stitches on the left needle. You should always have a total of 20 stitches between the two needles. As you progress through the row, keep sliding the stitches on the right needle down to prevent them from bunching up. Keep your knitting loose enough that the stitches slide easily along the needle.

7. When you have transferred all the stitches on your left needle to the right, you have completed one row of purling. Turn the work around, making the old right needle the new left one, and vice versa, and purl a few more rows for practice.

Stockinette Stitch

Now that you have mastered the two fundamental stitches of knitting, you will combine them into knitting's most basic pattern: stockinette stitch. In stockinette stitch, you simply alternate rows of knit stitches with rows of purl stitches. The result is a knitted piece with a smooth right side and a bumpy wrong side.

Try a practice swatch in stockinette stitch:

1. Cast on 20 stitches by the cable method, as described on pages 12–14.

2. Knit across the first row of stitches, as explained on pages 20–23.

3. Purl across the second row of stitches, as explained on pages 23–26.

4. Alternate knit and purl rows to create a swatch.

The right side of a stockinette swatch

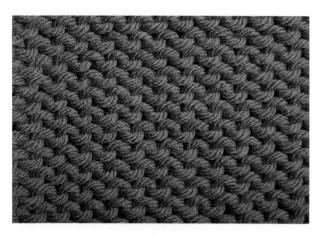

The wrong side of a stockinette swatch

TIP» Try to keep your stitches consistent in tension. Some beginning knitters purl more loosely than they knit. Controlling the tension with your index finger as you pull the yarn through the stitch is important. You will gain better control of this as you become more experienced.

Working Through the Back Loops (tbl)

Occasionally, a pattern will instruct you to knit or purl "through the back loops." This technique—which more accurately should be called working through the back of the loops—twists the stitches, and is sometimes used for decorative effects.

Knitting through the back loops (k tbl)

1. Insert your needle under the back strand of the next stitch, going through it in the opposite direction from how you would normally knit a stitch. If you think of the needle going into a stitch from left to right normally, this time it will go in from right to left. (Alternately, if you think of the stitch in vertical terms, with the needle ordinarily going in from below the loop, this time it will go in from above.)

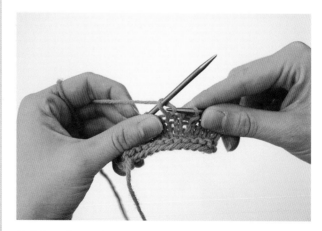

2. Wrap the working yarn around your needle (English style) or pick up the working yarn with your needle (Continental style) and pull it through the stitch.

Purling through the back loops (p tbl)

1. Insert your needle under the back strand of the next stitch, going through it in the opposite direction from how you would normally knit a stitch. If you think of the needle going into a stitch from right to left normally, this time it will go in from left to right. (In vertical terms, the needle ordinarily goes in from above the loop to purl; this time it will go in from below.) Purling through the back loop is a little more awkward than knitting through it.

2. Wrap the working yarn around your needle (English style) or pick up the working yarn with your needle (Continental style).

3. Pull the yarn through the stitch.

Knitting and purling through the back loops produce the same effect—stitches that are twisted at the base. You can see this effect in this swatch.

Shaping: Increases and Decreases

You could keep knitting on your practice swatch indefinitely, continuing to knit and purl on the same 20 stitches that you cast on. Eventually, you would produce a long, narrow piece, appropriate perhaps for a thin scarf or belt. But in knitting other garments such as sweaters and vests, it is necessary to change the shape of the garment; to either add or subtract stitches in order to make armholes, collars, or cuffs. You can also use increases and decreases for decorative purposes (see the Bayside Scarf on page 120). There are various methods of increasing and decreasing the number of stitches in a garment. The main ones are covered on the following pages.

Increases

Bar Increase

The simplest and most common increase method is called the bar increase. This increase is good for shaping a garment, as it leaves no hole in the finished fabric.

1. On a knit row, knit to the point in the row where you want to work the increase.

2. Knit the next stitch as usual, but do not slip it off the left needle.

3. With the stitch still on the left needle, insert the right needle into the stitch again, but this time from the back of the loop.

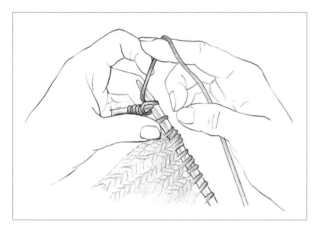

Make sure to insert the needle into the BACK of the loop.

4. Knit the stitch as usual, then slip both stitches off the left needle. The second stitch should have a small loop of yarn at its base, the "bar" of the increase's name.

A bar increase on a knit-side row. Note the horizontal bar at the base of the increased stitch.

To work a bar increase on a purl-side row:

1. On a purl row of your knitted swatch, purl to the point in the row where you want to work the increase.

2. Purl the next stitch, but do not slip it off the left needle.

3. With the stitch still on the left needle, insert the right needle up through the stitch again, but this time from the back of the loop.

4. Purl the stitch as usual, then slip both stitches off the left needle.

When working a bar increase on a purl-side row, you will see the "bar" only on the right side of the knitted piece.

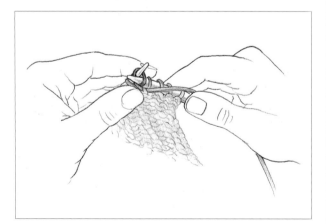

Make sure to insert the needle into the BACK of the loop.

Raised Increase

The raised increase is useful when adding stitches in the body or sleeves of a garment. Like the bar increase, it shows no hole and—even better—it is practically invisible in the finished garment.

1. On a knit row of your swatch, knit to the point in the row where you want to work the increase. Before you knit the next stitch, tilt your needles toward you so you can see the back of the knitting. Locate the stitch directly below the next stitch on your left needle.

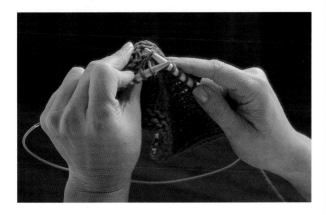

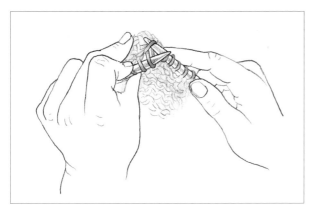

2. Insert the tip of your right needle into the back of the loop of this stitch.

3. Tilt the knitting back to normal position with the stitch on the right needle.

4. Knit through the stitch but do not slip it off the needle.

5. Knit the stitch on the left needle and slip it off the needle.

A raised increase on a knit-side row

To work a raised increase on a purl row:

1. On a purl row of your swatch, purl to the point in the row where you want to work the increase. Now locate the stitch directly below the next stitch on your left needle. (It's the "bump" at the base of the stitch.)

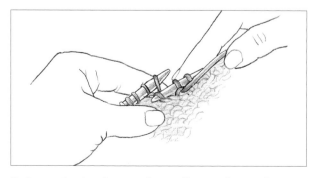

2. Insert the tip of your right needle into this stitch.

3. Bring the stitch into position and prepare to purl it.

4. Purl through the stitch but do not slip it off the needle.

5. Purl the stitch on the left needle and slip it off the needle.

A raised increase on a purl-side row as seen from the right side of the piece

Make One (M1)

This increase is commonly used in shaping garments. In this method, the increase is worked into the "ladder" between the two stitches from the previous row of knitting. Two different versions of the increase, the right slant and left slant, are typically used in conjunction with one another to provide a symmetrical increase.

Make One (Left Slant)

1. On a knit row of your swatch, knit to the point in the row where you want to work the increase. Before knitting the next stitch, gently spread the needles apart. Notice the strand of yarn that bridges the gap between these two stitches.

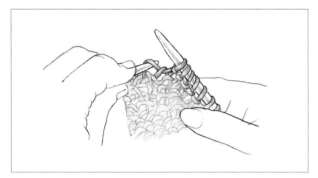

2. Insert the tip of the left needle (not the right needle) from front to back under this "ladder" and lift it onto the left needle.

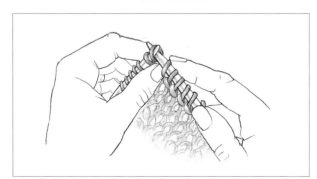

3. Insert the tip of the right needle through the back of the stitch.

4. Knit the stitch.

5. Slide the new stitch off the needle and knit the rest of the row as usual.

An M1 (left slant) increase on a knit-side row

To work this increase on a purl row:

1. Purl to the point in the row where you want to work the increase. Before purling the next stitch, gently spread the needles apart. Notice the strand of yarn that bridges the gap between these two stitches.

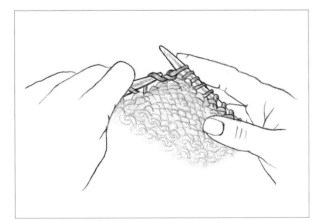

2. Insert the tip of the left needle from front to back under this "ladder" and lift it onto the left needle.

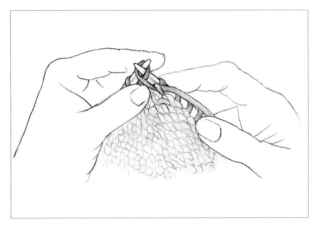

3. Insert the tip of the right needle through the back of the stitch.

4. Purl the stitch.

5. Slide the new stitch off the needle and purl the rest of the row as usual.

An M1 (left-slant) increase on a purl-side row as seen from the right side of the piece

NOTE » In this book, in cases when the direction of the increase matters, we will abbreviate the M1 increases as follows:

M1l Make one (left slant)
M1r Make one (right slant)

Make One (Right Slant)

1. On a knit row of your swatch, knit to the point in the row where you want to work the increase. Before knitting the next stitch, gently spread the needles apart. Notice the strand of yarn that bridges the gap between these two stitches.

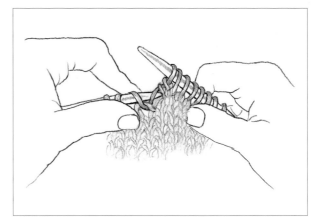

2. Insert the tip of the left needle (not the right needle) from back to front under this "ladder" and lift it onto the left needle.

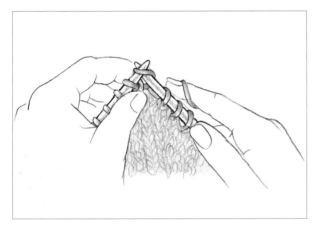

3. Insert the tip of the right needle through the front of the stitch.

4. Knit the stitch.

5. Slide the new stitch off the needle and knit the rest of the row as usual.

An M1 (right-slant) increase on a knit-side row

To work this increase on a purl row:

1. Purl to the point in the row where you want to work the increase. Before purling the next stitch, gently spread the needles apart. Notice the strand of yarn that bridges the gap between these two stitches.

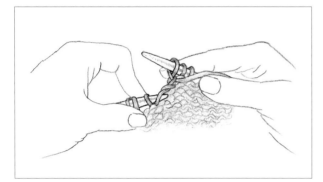

2. Insert the tip of the left needle from back to front under this "ladder" and lift it onto the left needle.

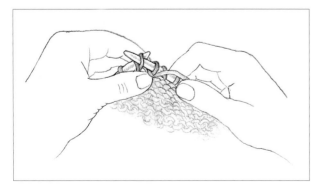

3. Insert the tip of the right needle through the front of the stitch.

4. Purl the stitch.

5. Slide the new stitch off the needle and purl the rest of the row as usual.

An M1 (right-slant) increase on a purl-side row as seen from the right side of the piece

NOTE » A fourth increase method, the yarn over, is used for decorative purposes. See page 71 to learn how to work a yarn over.

Decreases

Knit Two Together (k2tog)

This right-slanting decrease is usually used in conjunction with its mirror image, the left-slanting knit 2 together through back loops decrease (k2tog tbl—see page 43). A common use is in shaping a sock or mitten (see page 127 for an example of these two decreases used for mitten shaping).

1. On a knit row of your swatch, knit to the point in the row where you want to work the decrease.

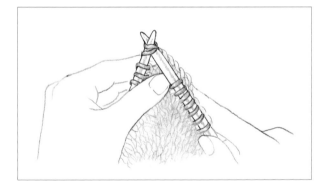

2. Insert the right needle into the next two stitches at the same time, as if to knit.

Needle inserted into both stitches as if to knit

3. Knit the two stitches together.

4. Slide the stitch onto the right needle and knit the rest of the row as usual.

A k2tog decrease on a knit-side row

Purl Two Together (p2tog)

To create a right-slanting decrease from a purl-side row, you can work a purl 2 together decrease (p2tog):

1. On a purl row of your swatch, purl to the point in the row where you want to work the decrease.

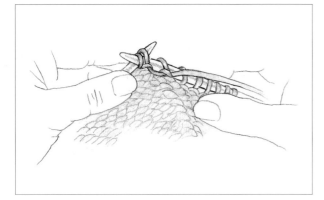

2. Insert the right needle into the next two stitches at the same time, as if to purl.

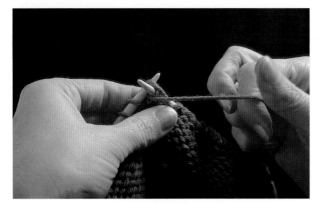

Needle inserted into both stitches as if to purl

3. Purl the two stitches together.

4. Slide the stitch off the needle and purl the rest of the row as usual.

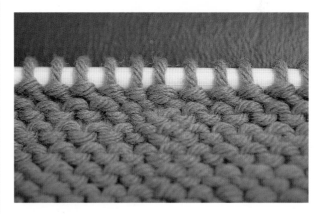

A p2tog decrease on a purl-side row

Purl Two Together Through Back Loops (p2tog tbl)

Another purl-side decrease is the purl 2 together through back loops (p2tog tbl), which creates a left-slanting decrease on the knit side.

1. On a purl row, purl to the point in the row that you want to work the decrease.

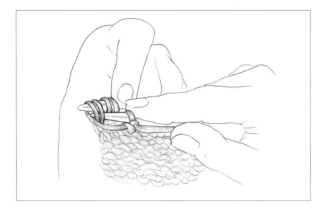

2. Bring the working yarn to the front, then turn the work toward you and push the right needle from right to left through the back of the loops.

Needle inserted through back of both loops

3. Purl the two stitches together through the backs of the stitches.

4. Slide the stitch off the needle and purl the rest of the row as usual.

A p2tog tbl decrease on a purl-side row

Slip, Slip, Knit (ssk)

This is a subtle, left-slanting decrease.

1. On a knit row of your swatch, knit to the point in the row that you want to work the decrease.

NOTE » The k2tog tbl decrease is frequently substituted for the ssk. The k2tog tbl is worked like the k2tog decrease (see page 40), except that you will insert the needle into the back of the loops of the two stitches. It achieves the same result as the ssk—both slant to the left.

2. Slip the next two stitches in the row by inserting the tip of your right needle into them as if to knit, but instead slide them onto the right needle without knitting them.

Both stitches slipped as if to knit

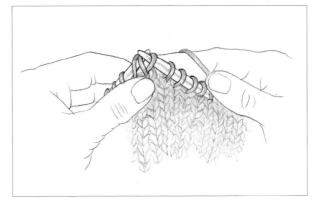

4. Knit the stitches together through the backs with the right needle.

3. Insert the tip of the left needle into the front of the two slipped stitches to hold them in place.

5. Slide the two stitches off the left needle and knit the rest of the row as usual.

An ssk decrease on a knit-side row

Slip, Knit, Pass (skp)

This is a less-than-subtle left-slanting decrease and is usually used only in lace patterns or textured stitches.

1. On a knit row of your swatch, knit to the point in the row that you want to work the decrease.

2. Slip the next stitch by inserting the tip of your right needle into it as if to knit, but instead slide it onto the right needle without knitting it.

3. Knit the next stitch of the row as usual.

4. Insert the tip of the left needle into the slipped stitch and lift it up.

5. Pass the slipped stitch over the knit stitch and slide it off the right needle. Try not to stretch the stitch if possible.

6. Knit the rest of the row as usual.

An skp decrease on a knit-side row

Slip, Purl, Pass (spp)

This purl-side decrease causes a right-slanting decrease on the knit side of the piece. It is worked very similarly to the slip, knit, pass above.

1. On a purl row, purl to the point in the row that you want to work the decrease.

2. Slip the next stitch by inserting the tip of your right needle into it as if to purl, but instead slide it onto the right needle without purling it.

3. Purl the next stitch of the row as usual.

4. Insert the tip of the left needle into the slipped stitch and lift it up.

6. Purl the rest of the row as usual.

An spp decrease on a purl-side row

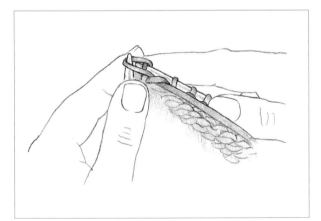

5. Pass the slipped stitch over the purl stitch and slide it off the right needle. Try not to stretch the stitch if possible.

Joining New Yarn

Whether you are knitting in one color or many, eventually you will run out of yarn and need to join a new ball. There are several different methods used to achieve this, but the simplest and most reliable is to secure the new yarn to the working yarn you have already been using by tying a knot.

2. Make a loop in the new yarn and slide it over the needle. Leave at least a 3-inch tail to work in later.

3. Pull the loop of new yarn through the first stitch.

1. At the beginning of a new row, cut the working yarn you have been using, making sure to leave at least a 3-inch tail. Have the yarn you want to join ready.

4. Continue to knit with the new yarn, being careful not to pull the tail through the first stitch.

5. After you've knit through four or five stitches in the row, turn the work to the back and fasten the two yarns with a square knot.

6. Pull the ends to secure the knot, then continue knitting the row as usual.

Picking Up Dropped Stitches

Even experienced knitters sometimes make mistakes. For beginners, the most common problem is "dropping" stitches. A dropped stitch is when a stitch accidentally slips off the needle and it unravels through the rows beneath it. Although this may look disastrous when you first spot it, it is in fact a fairly easy mistake to fix. You will need a crochet hook, slightly smaller than the thickness of the knitting needle you are using.

TIP » To minimize the problems caused by dropped stitches, recount the number of stitches on your needle frequently to make sure that you have not lost any stitches.

1. With the right side of the work toward you, visually trace the path of the dropped stitch down through the rows, noting the "ladders" it's created on the way.

2. Insert the crochet hook from front to back into the dropped stitch.

5. Remove the new stitch from the hook and hold it between your thumb and index finger.

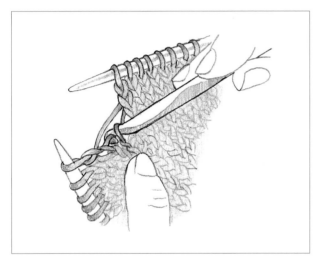

3. Pull the first ladder through the loop of the stitch.

6. Insert the crochet hook into this new stitch as in Step 2.

4. Continue pulling the ladder through the stitch.

7. Continue working your way up through the rows in this manner, pulling the ladders through the loop of the stitch until you reach the top.

8. Replace the loop onto the needle, making sure not to twist the stitch when you do so.

A completed repair job

TIP» To repair a dropped stitch on a purl row, simply turn the work to the knit side and correct it as described above.

Taking Out Stitches

There will be times when, despite your most concerted efforts, you will make a mistake in a pattern: you will forget to increase in a row or make a mistake that will throw off all the rows that follow. The best thing to do is to inspect your work often, counting your stitches and making sure that your pattern looks the way it should.

If you do find a mistake in a row that you have just completed, you can simply "unknit" the stitches in that row:

1. Identify the point in the row where the mistake was made (in this case, an errant purl stitch in a knit row, four stitches back).

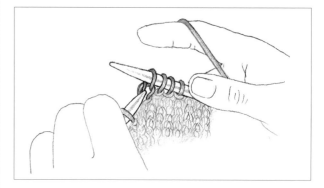

2. Insert the tip of the left needle into the stitch below the incorrect one.

3. Ease the working yarn out of the stitch and pull the right needle out.

Repeating Step 3

4. Return the "unknit" stitch to the left needle.

5. Repeat Steps 2–4 until you reach the mistake.

Repeating Step 4

6. Correct the stitch(es) and continue with the row.

Repeating Step 2

If you miss a mistake and continue to knit through subsequent rows, however, it is best to remove the stitches and reknit the rows. This is called unraveling or, more commonly, "ripping out."

1. Locate your mistake and note how many rows you need to remove to reach it (in this case, two purl stitches in the middle of the previous row).

2. Lay the piece flat and slip the stitches off the needle by pulling the needle out from left to right.

3. Gently pull the working yarn to unravel the stitches.

4. Stop when you reach one row above the point of your mistake.

5. Pull out the stitches in the last row one by one.

6. When you reach the point where the mistake appears, remove these stitches and correct them. Continue with the row according to the pattern.

Twisted Stitches

When placed on the needle correctly, a knit or purl stitch will form an upside-down U on the needle. The right side of the U will be to the front of the needle and the left side will be to the back. If a stitch is placed on the needle improperly, it is considered to be twisted, and must be fixed in order to ensure a clean, tight knitted piece. To fix a twisted stitch, simply remove it from the left needle with the point of the right needle (or vice versa) and replace it on the needle in the correct position. It is sometimes difficult for beginners to spot twisted stitches, but as you gain experience you will be able to see them right away.

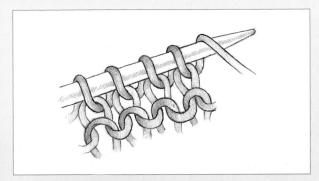

A row of correct knit stitches

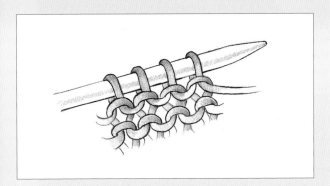

A row of correct purl stitches

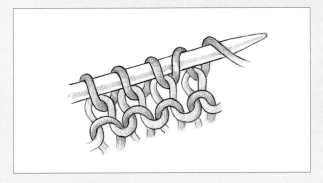

A twisted knit stitch

Binding Off

When you have completed your piece of knitting, you must secure the last row of stitches so they will not unravel. Binding off also secures stitches that are no longer required for a garment, such as at armholes or necklines.

TIP» It is common for beginning knitters to bind off too tightly, causing unsightly puckers along the edge of the garment. One way to avoid this is to bind off with a needle one or two sizes larger than the one you used to knit the rest of the piece.

1. On a knit row, knit the first two stitches of the row as usual.

4. Knit the next stitch and repeat Steps 2–3 to bind off the rest of the row.

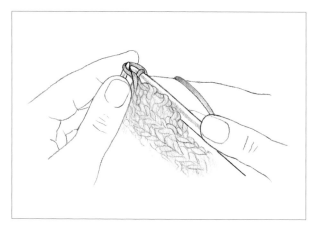

2. Using the point of the left needle, lift up the first knit stitch and pass it over the second stitch.

5. Continue binding off until you are left with only one stitch on your right needle.

3. Slide the stitch off the right needle.

6. Cut the working yarn, leaving a 3-inch tail.

The last stitch and tail

7. Pull the cut end through the final stitch to finish off. (You will learn what to do with this tail on page 56.)

A completed bound-off edge

To bind off on a purl-side row, repeat Steps 1–5 above, substituting purl stitches for knit stitches.

TIP» When binding off in ribbing or in any other pattern, adhere to the pattern when binding off the stitches: knit the knit stitches and purl the purl stitches.

Finishing

The term "finishing" is used to describe the various final steps you must take to complete your garment or knitted piece and make it ready to wear or display. No matter how well you complete the actual knitting, your garment will not look professional unless you pay careful attention to these finishing techniques. While you will no doubt be eager to finish your garment, fight the urge to rush through the finishing steps. The professional appearance of a well-finished garment will make you glad that you did.

Blocking

Blocking helps to even out the gauge of a finished knitted piece by relaxing the fibers of the yarn. While the piece is moist and pliable, you can adjust its size and shape slightly to fit the measurements specified in the pattern.

TIP» Depending on the type of project, some knitters do very minimal blocking. In the cabled vest in the photographs, for example, only the very edges of the front should be blocked to avoid flattening the cables that stand out from the texture. Additionally, you should never block ribbing that you want to remain elastic.

Steam Blocking

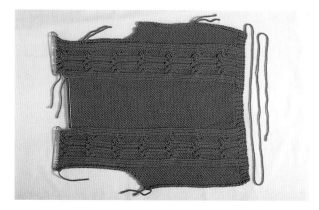

1. Lay the garment wrong-side-up on a clean, smooth, flat surface. A carpeted floor will do fine. Smaller pieces of knitting can be blocked on an ironing board. Use round-headed pins or T-pins to pin the garment to the surface on which it will be blocked. Measure the piece as you go to make sure that it will be blocked to fit the dimensions specified in the pattern.

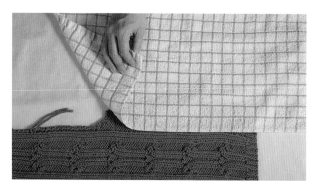

2. Place a clean press cloth over the section of the garment to be blocked.

3. Add water to your iron and set it to the steam setting. Hold the iron ½ inch above the surface of the garment and allow the steam to flow over the cloth and onto the garment. Allow the garment to remain pinned to the surface until it dries.

Wet Blocking

With this method, you simply pin the garment to the blocking surface and then use a fine-mist spray bottle to dampen the piece. Gently pat the surface of the garment to help the yarn fibers absorb the moisture. Adjust the shape or size of the garment as necessary, repin, and allow to lie flat until it is dry.

Seaming

In order to join together pieces of knitting into a finished garment, it is sometimes necessary to sew them together using a process known as seaming. It is best to seam pieces together using the tail of the yarn you left when you first cast on the piece to be joined. If you know that you will be seaming together a piece of knitting, make sure to leave a long enough tail to join it (a piece a little longer than the finished length of the edge should be adequate).

There are a number of different methods of seaming to choose from, but the most basic one, mattress stitch, will be shown here. This technique is worked one stitch in from the edge of the pieces to be joined together and is used on pieces that are knit in stockinette stitch.

1. Start by laying the two pieces to be joined right-side-up in front of you.

2. Thread the tail of the piece to be joined through a large tapestry needle.

NOTE » In the photos, a contrasting color of yarn is used to more effectively show the seam. In reality, the blue tail of the garment would be used to sew the seam.

3. Starting at the bottom of the piece without the tail (the piece on the left in the photo), insert the needle from wrong side to right side one stitch in from the corner.

4. Run the needle through the center of the first and second stitches of the first row of the piece with the tail, catching the two horizontal bars of yarn at the top of each stitch. Pull gently to tighten.

TIP » If you fail to leave a tail long enough to sew the entire seam of your garment, start with a new piece of yarn, leaving a long enough tail to weave in when you are finished sewing the seam.

5. On the other side of the seam (the piece without the tail), run the needle through the center of the first and second stitches, one row in from the edge.

6. Catch the two horizontal bars at the top of each stitch and pull gently to tighten.

7. On the side of the seam with the tail (the right piece), run the needle through the center of the first and second stitches, one row in from the edge. Catch the two horizontal bars at the top of each stitch and pull gently to tighten.

8. Continue in this fashion up the length of the seam.

9. At the end of the seam, weave in the remainder of the tail by weaving it through the stitches in the seam for at least 2 inches.

10. Cut the yarn close to the base of the last stitch.

Weaving in Ends

Once you have sewn up all the seams in your garment, the final step in finishing it will be to turn it inside out and weave all the remaining loose tail ends into seams or through nearby stitches to make sure that they are secured snugly before cutting them. All your tails should be at least 3 inches long to begin with, so you should have no trouble threading these through a tapestry needle and weaving them in.

2. Gently pull the needle all the way through the stitches, easing the yarn through as you go.

3. Pull snug to tighten, but don't pull so hard that the garment puckers.

1. Weave a tapestry needle under at least 2 inches of purl stitch bumps, then thread the tail of yarn through the needle's eye.

4. Holding the garment flat, cut the end about ⅛ of an inch from the last stitch the tail runs through.

5. Continue to weave in the rest of the loose tail ends. Check to make sure that none of the ends show through on the right side of the garment.

TIP» When knitting with more than one color, try to weave in the ends in a row of the same color as the tail end of the yarn.

Reading a Pattern

For the beginning knitter, knitting patterns can often be confusing. But once you know the basic information patterns communicate and what to do with it, they make much more sense. Take a look at the Biscayne Bay Shell pattern on page 156. Each section is identified and explained below.

> **TIP»** Make sure you read each sentence in the pattern in its entirety before starting to follow its instructions. Sometimes patterns contain more than one instruction per sentence.

Skill Level

The first piece of information in the patterns in this book is the skill level. This book, like many knitting books, uses the skill levels defined by the Craft Yarn Council; for a complete definition of the skills included under each level, see the table on page 179. Look at skill levels as general guidelines to help you understand what you're getting into in a pattern—not as strict indicators of what patterns you can and cannot attempt. There is a lot of variation possible within each level, and some patterns classified as more difficult may not be as challenging as you think. Take the skill level into account, but scan the pattern as well to see what skills are required and whether you understand how to do them.

Materials

The next few sections of the pattern indicate the materials needed for the project—yarn, needles, and notions (other tools such as stitch holders or yarn needles and trimmings such as buttons or zippers). Some patterns will specify brand names of yarns while others will indicate only the type of yarn (fingering, sport, worsted) that is needed; even if a specific yarn is mentioned, you can almost always substitute another yarn of the same weight and fiber type. If you are knitting a one-size garment such as a throw, a set quantity of yarn will be specified. If the pattern is for several sizes, the quantity will depend on the size you plan to knit. Needle sizes are given as a general guideline; you should use whatever size needle gives you the correct gauge (see pages 61 and 64), whether it is the one called for in the pattern or not.

> **TIP»** Make sure to purchase all the yarn you will need to complete your project at one time. Since yarn is usually dyed in batches (called dye lots), purchasing it at different times may result in having two skeins from different dye lots. The color can vary noticeably from dye lot to dye lot.

Finished Measurements

Most garment patterns provide a range of sizes. You will first need to obtain accurate measurements for yourself or the intended wearer and then consult the pattern's sizing chart to determine which size is most appropriate. You can refer to the general body measurement tables on pages 181–83 for a very general idea of the measurements you can expect from patterns that do not include a sizing chart.

> **TIP»** One good way to get measurements for a knitted piece is to take a similar garment (your favorite sweater, for example) and lay it on a flat surface for measurement. Remember that the actual size of sweaters and other similar garments is measured across the widest part of the garment; length is measured from the top of the shoulder to the lower edge of the garment, and sleeve length is measured through the center of the sleeve from the shoulder seam to the cuff. Once you have the measurements of your favorite sweater, you can check them against the "actual" measurements in the pattern to see which size most closely corresponds with your ideal fit.

Once you've decided which size garment you want to knit, you will be able to determine how much yarn you will need and how many stitches you will initially need to cast on. Patterns usually use brackets to indicate additional sizes. The main size is listed first and subsequent larger sizes are listed in brackets following it: 32 [34, 36, 38]. When reading the pattern, you need to read only the number that corresponds in sequence to the size you are knitting. In other words, a pattern will say: "Cast on 64 [68, 72, 76] stitches." If you are knitting a size-36 garment, then you need to follow the second number within the brackets, or 72 stitches. Increases and decreases are also indicated in this manner, as are various other instructions such as repeating rows: "Repeat these two rows 6 [6, 8, 8] more times." It may be easier for you to read the pattern if you use a colored highlighter to indicate which numbers correspond to which size in the pattern. (If you knit the pattern again in a different size, choose a different color of highlighter.)

Gauge

Gauge refers to how tightly or loosely you knit, and it is essential to proper garment fit. Because of individual differences between knitters, two knitters working the same stitch pattern on the same size of needles with the same yarn may end up with very different-sized pieces. Always work a small test piece (called a gauge swatch) to make sure your knitting matches that of the person who wrote the pattern. If your knitting is tighter than the pattern calls for (i.e. the gauge swatch is smaller than it should be), try a larger needle; if your knitting is looser (i.e. the gauge swatch is bigger than it should be), go down a needle size. In this pattern, a swatch 20 stitches wide by 24 rows tall, worked in stockinette stitch, should measure 4 inches by 4 inches. For complete instructions on knitting a gauge swatch and checking your gauge, see page 64.

Abbreviations in Patterns

Knitting patterns use abbreviations to save space when writing out instructions. Although they may seem a bit confusing at first, the more you knit the more they will become familiar. See page 185 for a list of the most common knitting abbreviations. Patterns that use unusual stitches often include a section giving the abbreviations used for these stitches (in this book, these will be found under "Special Stitches").

Asterisks (*) are often used in patterns to indicate instructions that need to be repeated. An asterisk will mark the beginning of a portion of the sequence that should be worked more than once. For example, "*k1, p1, k1, p5; rep from * to end" means that, after you've completed the sequence once, you repeat it again and again until you reach the end of the row or round. Brackets and parentheses are also used for a similar purpose. For example, "[k1, p1] twice" means k1, p1, k1, p1.

Example:

Row 5: K4, *[k2tog] twice, [yo, k1] 3 times, yo, [sl1, k1, psso] twice, k1; rep from * to last 3 sts, k3—55 sts.

To follow this pattern, begin by knitting the first 4 stitches. Next, do two k2tog decreases in a row. Yarn over, knit the next stitch; yarn over again, then knit the next stitch; yarn over a third time, and knit the next stitch, followed by one more yarn over. Next work two slip, knit, pass decreases in a row, and then knit one more stitch. Return to the asterisk and work the instructions following it again (starting with the two k2togs in a row); keep repeating these instructions until only 3 stitches are left. Knit these last 3 stitches. At the end of the row, you should have 55 stitches on your needle.

Reading a Chart

Charts provide a visual representation of the stitches in a repeat and give a better indication of how the finished motif will look. Although they may look overwhelming at first, once mastered, charts offer an enhanced way to view a pattern.

The practice of representing stitches in graphic form is known as Symbolcraft. Different stitches are represented by different symbols. Each symbol represents how the stitch will look on the right-hand side of the work. Each square of the chart equals one stitch. Each line of the chart equals one row of knitting.

For flat knitting, charts are read from right to left on right-side rows and from left to right on wrong-side rows, and charts are usually numbered as such. All charts are read from bottom to top.

Below is an example of the Symbolcraft for this sample 10-stitch pattern (knit flat):

Row 1 (RS): P4, k1, p1, k4
Row 2: P3, k2, p2, k3
Row 3: P2, k2, p1, k1, p2, k2
Row 4: P1, k2, p2, k2, p2, k1
Row 5: K2, p3, k3, p2
Row 6: K1, p4, k4, p1

In circular knitting, the chart is always read from right to left. The chart below is for the 12-stitch repeat of Pattern I for the Tracy Ridge Hat:

Rnd 1 (RS): Purl.
Rnd 2: *(P1, k1, p1) into next st, k3tog; rep from * to end.
Rnd 3: Purl.
Rnd 4: *K3tog, (p1, k1, p1) into next st; rep from * to end.

Patterns with colorwork often use charts to represent the color patterns—each square of the chart is filled in with the color for the corresponding stitch. (See the Big Rock Socks, page 150, for examples of color charts and more information on how to follow them.)

More complex patterns are represented in the same way, just on a larger scale. Charts of larger patterns also make it easier to see the texture of a repeated motif. The chart for Pattern II of the Tracy Ridge Hat, for example, provides a very good graphic representation of the cabled motif as it recurs throughout the pattern.

Sample 10-stitch pattern

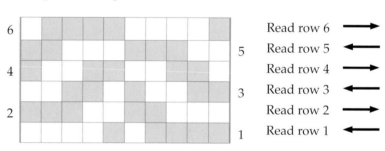

Pattern I—12 sts

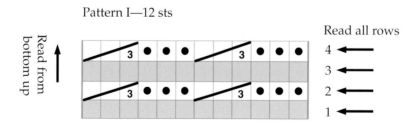

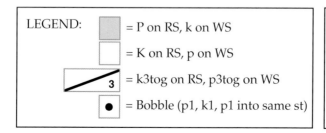

LEGEND:
= P on RS, k on WS
= K on RS, p on WS
3 = k3tog on RS, p3tog on WS
● = Bobble (p1, k1, p1 into same st)

NOTES:
In circular knitting, read all patterns R to L.
Read all patterns bottom to top.

Some knitters prefer reading charts to written instructions. Some patterns provide both charts and written instructions for those who prefer one method over the other. The ability to read both will prepare you to work with whatever representation the pattern designer chooses.

LEGEND:

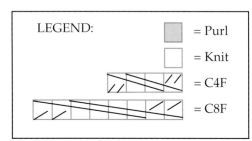

= Purl

= Knit

= C4F

= C8F

NOTES:

In circular knitting, read all patterns R to L.

Read all patterns bottom to top.

Read all rows

Pattern II—28 sts

Read from bottom up

Gauge

Gauge is without a doubt the single most important consideration when undertaking a knitting project. Unfortunately, however, in their eagerness to begin a new project, many knitters pay only a fleeting bit of attention to gauge or, worse yet, ignore it all together.

Every knitting pattern provides you with a gauge, a fixed number of stitches and rows per inch that are required to ensure that the piece or garment will fit properly. Depending on how loose or tight you knit, you may need to make adjustments in order to match this gauge.

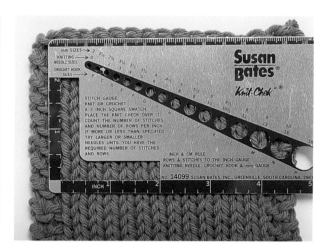

1. Knit a 4 x 4-inch square sample swatch with the needles and yarn you plan to use for the garment. Work the swatch in the pattern specified for the garment (garter stitch, stockinette stitch, seed stitch, etc.). If no pattern is specified, work the swatch in stockinette stitch (knit one row, purl one row). Make sure to cast on at least four more stitches than you need to make a 4-inch swatch, since edge stitches are an unreliable measure of gauge. Bind off.

2. Measure your gauge on the swatch by laying the piece flat on a smooth, hard surface such as a table. Lay a gauge check along the edge of the piece. Count the number of stitches that fall within the 2-inch range. Each "V" in stockinette stitch represents a stitch.

3. Lay the gauge check vertically across the center of the swatch and count the number of rows. Each "V" in stockinette stitch represents a row.

Compare your number of stitches and rows with the gauge stated on your pattern. If you have exactly the right number of stitches and rows, then you are ready to start your project. If not, then you need to make a few adjustments:

- If your swatch has too many stitches or rows, your knitting is tighter than it should be, and you need to increase the size of your needles to obtain the correct gauge.
- If your swatch has too few stitches or rows, your knitting is looser than it should be, and you need to decrease the size of your needles to obtain the correct gauge.

Repeat Steps 1–3 with either larger or smaller needles. Go up or down by a single size: for example, if your swatch had too many stitches when knit on a size 6 needle, try again on a size 7.

TIP» The type of yarn you use has a great deal to do with the gauge. If you are unable to find the exact yarn specified in the pattern, then you will need to try to find a substitute yarn as close in weight and fiber content as possible. Most yarns include a gauge on the ball band; try to come as close as possible to matching the original yarn's gauge.

CHAPTER 2

Skills for Texture and Color

Knitting With Two Skeins of Yarn

One of the simplest ways to create an exciting texture or color combination in a project is by knitting with two different skeins of yarn. Some patterns call for you to hold two strands of one kind of yarn together to achieve an effect like using a thicker version of the same yarn. More unusual results can be achieved by combining yarns of varying weights, textures, and colors. Match a delicate mohair with a more substantial DK weight, or combine a novelty eyelash with a slubby cotton. You can experiment with these combinations in the simple garter stitch scarves that have recently become popular.

A solid mohair combined with a variegated boucle produces this wonderful texture.

A metallic-thread novelty yarn combined with a variegated spiral yarn creates this interesting color pattern.

Swatching for Texture and Color

It's not always easy to tell what a yarn will look like when knitted up—and this is even more true when you're combining two or more different yarns. When selecting yarn for a pattern such as the Tionesta Lake Throw (page 118), which uses several different yarn types and colors, it's a good idea to knit a swatch or two to find the perfect combination. The instructions here illustrate swatching for the Tionesta Lake Throw, which uses three yarn selections (A, B—which is two strands held together—and C); you can create similar swatches when working on your own projects to experiment with combining different colors and textures of yarn.

1. Cast on 15 stitches with A. Knit Rows 1 and 2 of the pattern. Cut the yarn at the end of each row, leaving a 6- to 8-inch tail. As you join yarn at the beginning of each row, do not secure it with a knot; simply pin down the loose yarn with your finger and knit the first few stitches carefully. (This will also give you more flexibility to adjust the length of the tail to match the previous ones.) You will be knotting the tails of the yarns below to secure the fringe (see Step 5).

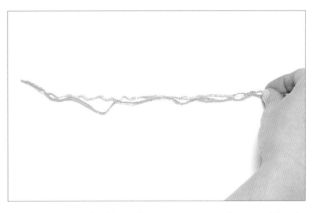

2. Prepare B by holding the rayon yarn and cotton blend together.

3. Knit Rows 3 and 4 with B, holding the two yarns together. Don't forget to cut the yarn at the end of each row for the fringe.

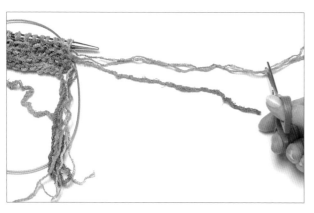

4. Knit Rows 5 and 6 with A, then 7 and 8 with B, cutting the yarn at the end of each row for the fringe.

The swatch at the end of Row 8, with A and B.

5. At the end of Row 8, tie the tail of this row together with the tail from Row 6 (A) with a loose overhand knot. Go back and secure previous rows' tails in the same fashion and continue to do so moving forward.

6. Following the pattern, knit Rows 9 and 10 with C, the blue mohair blend, followed by Rows 11 and 12 with A.

The swatch at the end of Row 12, with combined yarns so far.

The swatch with all 5 yarns introduced

8. Complete the swatch with Rows 21–24, using A and B. Bind off loosely.

The finished swatch

7. Knit Rows 13–18 with B, A, and B as written, then introduce D, the multicolor mohair blend, in Rows 19 and 20.

Slip-Stitch Knitting

The basic technique for slip-stitch knitting is the same whether you use it with one skein of yarn or two. The instructions that follow will teach you how to bring forward a second color of yarn, but the technique can be applied the same way when using just one color. If you are working in just one color of yarn (or variegated yarn from the same skein, as is the case with the Bamboo Forest Sweater on page 168), skip Step 1 and start with Step 2. You will create the same horizontal bars in your garment, but they will appear in the same color as the rest of the stitches in the garment.

3. Slip the next stitch as if to purl.

1. Join the new color and knit across the row to the point you want to bring forward the old color (in this case, the old color is blue and the new color is yellow).

2. Bring the working yarn to the front of the work.

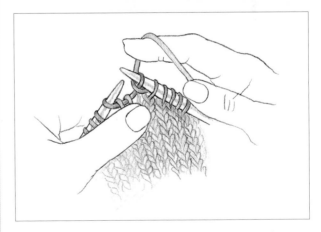

4. Return the working yarn to the back of the work.

69

5. Knit the next stitch in the row as usual.

6. As you can see, this creates a horizontal bar at the bottom of the slipped stitch in the new color, while the stitch itself is in the old color.

To slip a stitch with the horizontal bar visible on the wrong side of the work (and no bar visible on the front):

1. Keeping the working yarn to the back of the work, slip the next stitch as if to purl.

2. Knit the next stitch in the row as usual.

3. There is no horizontal bar at the base of the slipped stitch, but a bar in the new color is visible at the base of the slipped stitch on the wrong side of the work.

Yarn Over

The beautiful lace patterns of many knitting projects (such as the Bayside Scarf, page 120) are created by a simple stitch called a yarn over (yo). While this method is technically an increase, adding an extra stitch to the row, it is not usually used for increasing because it creates a hole, or eyelet, in the piece; however, this effect is perfect for creating lace patterns! When you want to keep the number of stitches in the row constant, the yarn over is balanced out with a decrease elsewhere in the row. In the examples that follow, the yo is immediately followed by a k2tog or a p2tog decrease in order to maintain a constant number of stitches in the row.

English-Style Yarn Over between Two Knit Stitches

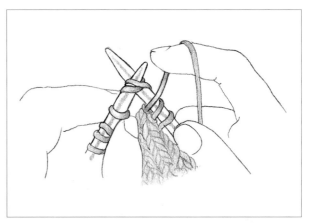

1. Knit the row up to the point where you will make the yarn over. Bring the yarn to the front and wrap it from front to back around the right needle.

2. Work a k2tog decrease immediately following the yo increase. Hold the yarn over in place on the right needle with your index finger as you work the decrease.

A yo increase paired with a k2tog decrease creates a "hole" in the knitting, which is often used in lace patterns.

Continental-Style Yarn Over between Two Knit Stitches

1. Knit to the point where you will make the yarn over. Pull the working yarn to the back and hold it in place with your index finger.

The end result of a yo + k2tog decrease is the same, whether you use the Continental or English method.

TIP» When doing a yarn over between a knit and a purl stitch, be sure to bring the yarn to the front between the needles after the knit stitch, then forward by carrying it over the top of the right needle and forward. If you fail to do this, it will not create an additional stitch. Similarly, when doing a yarn over between a purl and a knit stitch, make sure to bring the yarn to the back by carrying it over the top of the right needle.

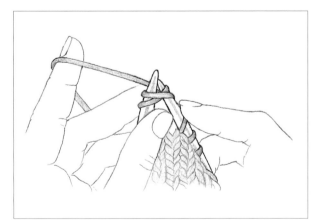

2. Continue holding down the yo with your index finger as you work the k2tog decrease.

English-Style Yarn Over between Two Purl Stitches

1. Purl the row up to the point where you will make the yarn over. Bring the yarn to the back over the top of the needle and then toward the front between the two needles.

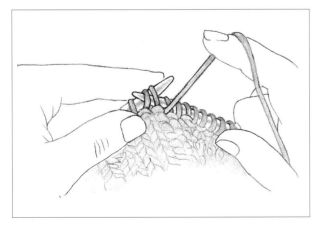

2. Work a p2tog decrease immediately following the yo increase. Hold the yarn over in place on the right needle with your index finger as you work the decrease.

A yo increase paired with a p2tog decrease

Continental-Style Yarn Over between Two Purl Stitches

1. Purl the row up to the point where you will make the yarn over. Wrap the yarn from front to back around the right needle. Hold the yarn in place at the front of the work with your thumb.

73

SKILLS FOR TEXTURE AND COLOR

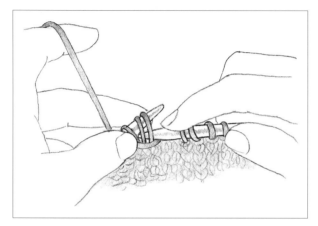

2. Continue holding down the yo with your thumb as you work the p2tog decrease.

A yo + p2tog decrease worked Continental style

Shaping with Lace— Placing Decreases

Sometimes in projects with lace patterns, the pattern will tell you to decrease but not specify exactly where to place the decreases (for an example, see the neck shaping of the Twin Lakes Cover-Up on page 138). Knowing where to place the decreases without destroying the lace pattern can be tricky. It may help to think of decreasing as eliminating stitches from the lace pattern from the right edge. As you eliminate these edges you still need to maintain the vertical integrity of the lace pattern.

1. Cast on 20 stitches and work 4 rows of stockinette to start your swatch. Work the first 6 rows of the lace pattern for the garment (here we are using the Twin Lakes Cover-Up lace pattern), but with a knit stitch at each edge:

Row 1 (RS): K1 (edge stitch), * yo, sl1, k2tog, psso, yo, k3; rep from * to last stitch, knit (edge stitch).
Row 2 and all even rows: Purl.

2. Knit the edge stitch on the swatch.

3. To make the decrease, omit the yarn over from the pattern, and continue by slipping the next stitch.

4. Then knit the next 2 stitches together and pass the slipped stitch over, as in the pattern.

5. Now work the yarn over and continue with the row as printed. The finished row will have 19 stitches.

6. Purl Row 2 (wrong side). Then on the next right-side row, you will decrease again. You have now eliminated the edge stitch, so you will start by slipping the first stitch in the row.

7. Knit the next 2 stitches together and pass the slipped stitch over.

8. Work the yarn over and continue with the row as printed. The finished row will have 18 stitches.

9. Purl the next row (wrong side). Then on the next right-side row, you will decrease again. You have eliminated the first lace section, so in order to maintain the integrity of the pattern, you need to work your decrease before reaching the knit 3 section: slip the first stitch in the row, knit the next stitch, and pass the slipped stitch over this single knit stitch.

10. Continue with the pattern (knit 3), then work the next lace section as the pattern indicates. The finished row will have 17 stitches.

To continue decreasing, continue eliminating stitches from the right-hand edge one at a time, always working to maintain the vertical integrity of the lace pattern.

Cables

Cables are a distinctive pattern, seen often in traditional Aran knitting. Cables are created by twisting a group of stitches over another group of stitches, done by placing the stitches to be twisted on a separate needle designed for the purpose. Cables are crossed from left to right (a left cable) or from right to left (a right cable) and can contain groups of two, three, or more stitches. Left twists are followed by right twists in the pattern to give the cable its distinctive twining look.

To twist a 4-stitch cable to the left:

1. On a right-side row of a swatch, work to the position where you want to place the first cable.

2. Slip the next 2 stitches, as if to purl them, onto the cable needle.

Two stitches slipped purlwise onto a cable needle

3. Holding the cable needle at the front, knit the next 2 stitches in the row with the cable needle holding the 2 slipped stitches still at the front.

4. Return the 2 stitches on the cable needle to the left needle, slipping them one by one.

5. Knit the returned stitches as usual.

6. Repeat this pattern as often as is specified in the pattern. Use a stitch counter to keep track of rows.

Cable twisted to the left

To twist a 4-stitch cable to the right, follow Steps 1–2 above, but instead of holding the cable needle at the front, hold it at the back. Then, as you did with Steps 3–5 above, knit the next 2 stitches in the row with the cable needle at the back and then return the 2 stitches on the cable needle to the left needle and knit them. Repeat this pattern as often as is specified in the pattern. Use a stitch counter to keep track of rows.

Cable twisted to the right

The completed cable pattern—twisted to the left, then to the right

Cable Abbreviations

There is a different abbreviation for every cable, depending on how many stitches are involved and what direction you're twisting them in. It can be confusing, but once you learn the general system, it's not so bad. While there are various systems for how to abbreviate cable directions, the most common is C + [number of stitches] + [F or B]:

C2F = Slip 1 st to a cable needle and hold in front of the work. Knit 1 st from the left needle, then knit the 1 st from the cable needle.

C2B = Slip 1 st to a cable needle and hold in back of the work. Knit 1 st from the left needle, then knit the 1 st from the cable needle.

C4F = Slip 2 sts to a cable needle and hold in front of the work. Knit 2 sts from the left needle, then knit the 2 sts from the cable needle.

C4B = Slip 2 sts to a cable needle and hold in back of the work. Knit 2 sts from the left needle, then knit the 2 sts from the cable needle.

C6F = Slip 3 sts to a cable needle and hold in front of the work. Knit 3 sts from the left needle, then knit the 3 sts from the cable needle.

C6B = Slip 3 sts to a cable needle and hold in back of the work. Knit 3 sts from the left needle, then knit the 3 sts from the cable needle.

Just remember that the number is the total number of stitches in the cable (not the number of stitches to move to the cable needle); the direction (F for front or B for back) is where you move the cable needle to once you have the stitches on it.

Ruffles

Ruffles are easy to make and can be tailored to fit the length of any garment's edge. Simply multiply the final desired stitches by 3; this gives you the number of stitches to cast on. For example, for the Twin Lakes Hat, you cast on 243 (261, 279) stitches to create a ruffle that matches a finished edge of 81 (87, 93) stitches (after Round 7).

You can control the degree to which the ruffle curls by adjusting the groupings of stitches in the decreases. See how this works by creating two swatches.

Cast on 20 stitches and work a 4-row garter stitch border. To create a gently curling ruffle, follow this pattern:

1. **Row 1 (RS):** *Knit 3 then knit 2 together. Repeat from *. The finished row will have 16 stitches.

2. Purl the wrong-side row. On the right-side row, * knit 2, then knit 2 together. Repeat from *. The finished row will have 12 stitches.

3. Purl the wrong-side row. On the right-side row, * knit 1, then knit 2 together. Repeat from *. The finished row will have 8 stitches.

4. Purl the wrong-side row. On the right-side row, * knit 2 together. Repeat from *.

5. The finished row will have 4 stitches.

To make a more quickly curling ruffle, you need to work decreases only, with no knit stitches in between. Cast on 20 stitches and work a 4-row garter stitch border.

1. **Row 1 (RS):** *Knit 2 together. Repeat from *. The finished row will have 10 stitches.

2. Purl the wrong-side row. On the right-side row, * knit 2 together. Repeat from *.

3. The finished row will have 5 stitches.

Compare the two finished ruffles:

The gently curling ruffle

The more quickly curling ruffle

You can also shorten or lengthen a ruffle by adjusting the number of knit and purl rows between the decrease rows. For a shorter ruffle, include fewer rows between the decreases; for a longer ruffle, add more.

Stranded Colorwork

Stranded colorwork, often mistakenly referred to as Fair Isle knitting, involves knitting with two colors of yarn at once, carrying the unused color across the back of the work until you need it again. To avoid long strands of yarn across the back of the garment, the yarn is usually carried, or wrapped, by securing it with the yarn currently being worked. This also prevents the second color from showing through the front of the piece and prevents the finished piece from puckering.

Since the swatch demonstrated below is knit flat, you will learn how to both knit and purl in this fashion, wrapping the carries as you go. For projects that are knit in the round in stockinette stitch, you will only need to use the knitting part of this process.

For this swatch, you will practice by knitting Pattern I from the Big Rock Socks. Note, however, that since it will be knit flat rather than in the round, you will need to work the even rows in purl stitch in the reverse order:

Row 1: K7B, k3A, k1B, k3A
Row 2: P2A, p3B, p2A, p7B
Row 3: K1B, k2A, k1B, k2A, k1B, k1A, k5B, k1A
Row 4: P7B, p3A, p1B, p3A
Row 5: K2A, k3B, k2A, k7B
Row 6: P1B, p2A, p1B, p2A, p1B, p1A, p5B, p1A

What is Fair Isle Knitting?

Fair Isle knitting is a specific type of stranded colorwork that originated on (you guessed it) Fair Isle, off the coast of Scotland. True Fair Isle knitting uses only Shetland wool and typically is characterized by color changes in both the foreground and background colors. "X" and "O" motifs are common. Stranded colorwork uses the same two-handed technique but encompasses patterns of all kinds.

Round 1: Knit Side

1. Cast on 18 stitches. Work 2 garter stitch edge stitches on either side of the swatch (all edge stitches should be knit in B). Knit 4 rows of stockinette stitch.

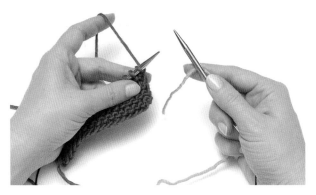

2. As you begin Round 1, hold Color A (blue) in your left hand and Color B (gold) in your right hand.

3. With B tacked down on the right needle with your right thumb, knit the 2 garter stitch edge stitches with A.

4. Insert the right needle into the next stitch and prepare to introduce B by tacking it down between your left thumb on the front of the swatch and your left middle finger on the back of the swatch. Wrap the working end around your right index finger to establish tension.

5. Wrap B around the left needle as if to knit (English style) and knit the stitch.

6. Knit the next stitch the same way.

7. On the third stitch, you will work a carry. Insert the needle into the stitch as to prepare to knit, then pull A over the top of the right needle, keeping the tension nice and tight with your left index finger.

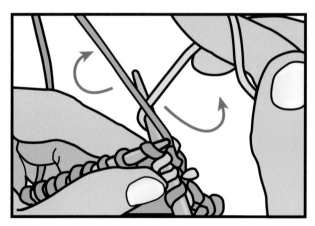

8. Now, wrap B around the right needle as if to knit, keeping A overtop the right needle.

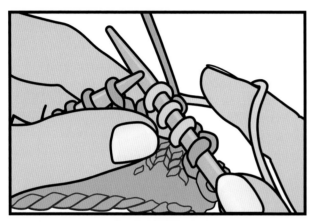

9. Back out A, pulling through only B, leaving A at the back, anchored to the stitch.

10. Knit the fourth stitch with B.

The carry worked on the third stitch from the back of the swatch

11. Knit the fifth stitch, and then on the sixth stitch, work another carry.

The completed carry on the sixth stitch

12. Work the seventh stitch with B.

13. To work the eighth stitch with A, insert the needle into the next stitch as if to knit and then wrap the yarn with the left hand as to knit Continental style.

As you prepare to knit the eighth stitch with A, it is important to maintain tension with B.

14. Knit the stitch Continental style.

TIP» When working with the yarn in your left hand, you should be "picking" the yarn through the stitch (Continental style); when holding the yarn in your right hand, you should be "throwing" it around the needle, then pulling through (English style).

15. Knit the ninth stitch with A.

16. Work a carry on the tenth stitch, but this time carrying B by backing out A, pulling through only B.

> **NOTE»** You need to work a carry after knitting 3 stitches in a new color; since you switched from B to A on stitch 7, you will work the carry on stitch 10.

17. Knit stitch 11 with B, remembering to maintain proper tension on A with your left hand.

18. Switch back to A and knit stitches 12, 13, and 14, working a carry on stitch 14.

19. Knit the 2 edge stitches in B.

The right side of finished Round 1

The wrong side of finished Round 1, showing the carries

Round 2: Purl Side

1. Knit the 2 edge stitches in A, then purl stitches 1 and 2 of the pattern. Remember, since you are holding A in your left hand, you will need to purl Continental style.

2. On stitch 3, switch to B and purl the next stitch English style.

3. Purl stitch 4.

4. On stitch 5, you will work the carry. First, insert the right needle into the next stitch as if to purl.

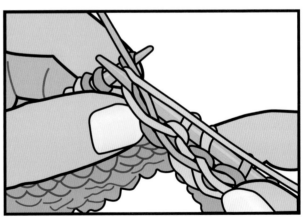

5. Next, keeping A overtop, wrap B underneath as if to purl (English style).

7. Switch to A and purl stitches 6 and 7.

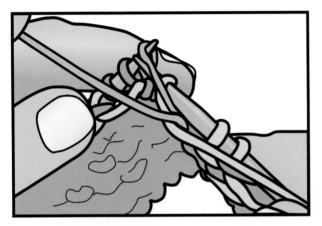

6. Now back A out and pull through only B.

8. Switch to B and purl stitches 8 and 9, then work a carry on stitch 10.

The completed carry on stitch 5

The completed carry on stitch 10

9. Purl stitches 11 and 12 with B and then work another carry on stitch 13.

10. Purl stitch 14 of the pattern.

11. Knit the two edge stitches in B.

The right side of completed Round 2

The wrong side of completed Round 2, showing the carries

The right side of completed Round 6

The wrong side of completed Round 6, showing the carries

Intarsia

Intarsia is another method of colorwork, ideal for knitting large blocks of color. While stranded colorwork is good for patterns with intricate or frequent color changes, it is not well suited for a large area of a single color within another color—carrying the yarn not in use behind the block of the other color reduces the elasticity of the fabric and yields long strings in the back of the work that can snag. Intarsia is perfect for patterns with large areas of solid color like this. However, intarsia can only be worked flat (in rows); for patterns worked in the round, you'll need to do stranded colorwork.

To work intarsia, you will need a separate ball of yarn for each pool of color. For example, to knit the color pattern shown below, you would need three balls of color A and two balls of color B.

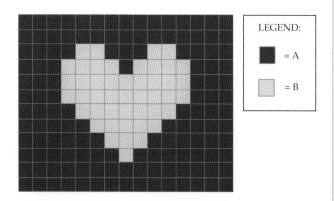

LEGEND:

■ = A

▨ = B

For small areas of intarsia, you may only need a small amount of yarn. Many knitters use bobbins to hold these small amounts of yarn; others wind the yarn around a business card or scrap of cardboard, or simply wrap it around itself. For very small pools of color, you may find it easier to just cut a short length of yarn and leave it hanging down the back of the work. Any method that helps you manage the multiple yarns without tangling them is fine.

1. Work up to the point where you start the new color (color B, here).

2. Join color B as you normally would and work as many stitches as required by the pattern in that color.

3. When you get to where you need to go back to the original color (color A), join a new ball or bobbin of that color and continue.

The end of the first row of intarsia.

4. On the next row, when you reach the intarsia portion, lay the working color A yarn over the color B yarn.

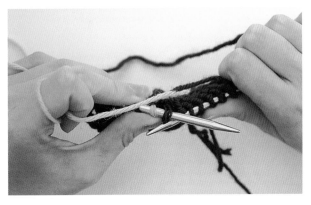

5. Pick up color B (past where A goes over it, so that B comes up and around A) and knit the next stitch with it. (To prevent holes in your work, give the end of A a small tug after the first stitch of B is knit, to tighten everything up.) Work all the stitches in B shown on the chart.

6. When you reach the end of the color B section, change to the first ball of A in the same way: lay the color B yarn over the original color A yarn before picking that yarn up and continuing to the end of the row.

The end of the second intarsia row.

7. The process is the same on the purl side. Purl up to the first color change. Lay the working yarn over the new color.

8. Pick up the new color below where the yarns cross and bring it up and around the old color. Purl the stitch with the new color. Continue in the same way across the row.

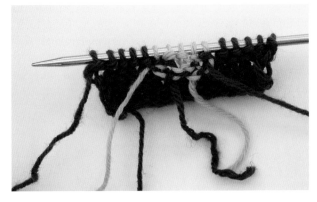

The end of the third row.

9. Continue to knit the design, always laying the old yarn over the new yarn every time you switch from one color to another. This twists the yarns together at the joints between blocks of color and prevents gaps in the work.

The back of the work. Once you finish the project, you will weave in all the loose ends in the intarsia section.

10. When you finish the intarsia section, tie off the extra yarn as you normally would and continue with a single ball of the main color.

The finished intarsia block.

CHAPTER 3

Skills for Building and Finishing Projects

Knitting in the Round on Circular Needles

Knitting in the round produces a seamless, tubular piece of knitting that is perfect for hats, socks, or sleeves. There are two methods of knitting in the round; one requires a circular needle, the other a set of double-pointed needles.

Circular needles are basically the tips of regular knitting needles joined by a thin, flexible strand of plastic. Stitches are knit on the tips of the needles in the usual fashion, then slid off the needles and onto the plastic as they are pushed around the circle. Circular needles come

in various sizes and lengths: 12, 16, 20, 24, 32, and 40-inch lengths are available. Always use the length of needle that your pattern indicates. Knitting on a longer needle will stretch the stitches and distort the final piece.

1. Using a 16-inch circular needle, cast on the required number of stitches using the cable method in the same manner you cast on with straight needles. The stitches will slide around the bend of the circle. Take care not to pull or stretch them.

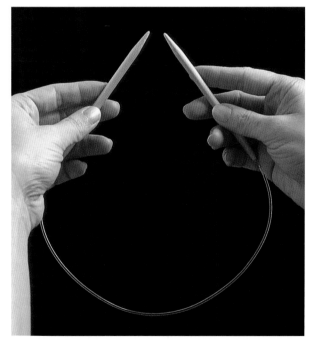

A circular needle

2. Insert a plastic marker over the tip of the right needle so you'll know where the round begins and ends.

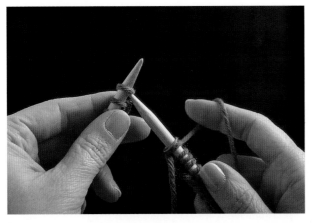

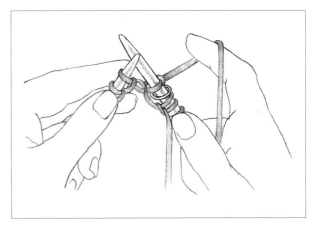

3. Hold the circular needle with the first cast-on stitch in your left hand and insert the needle into the first stitch.

4. Knit into the first stitch, making sure the tension is high enough that the stitch is flush against the needle before sliding it off.

Properly positioned stitches

Twisted stitches

Twisted Stitches

Before you start knitting in the round, it is essential to make sure that your stitches are not twisted on the needle. Lay the needle down on a flat surface and turn all stitches in so the cast-on edge faces the center of the circle. If any stitches are twisted, correct them now. After you have knit the circle together, there is no way to fix twisted stitches other than removing them and starting again.

5. Continue knitting in this fashion, sliding the stitches around the needle as you go.

6. When you reach the end of the row . . .

. . . pass the marker from the tip of the left needle . . .

. . . to the tip of the right.

One completed row of circular knitting

TIP›› Unlike on straight needles, in which you turn the work from right to wrong side, when working on circular needles the right side of the knitting is always facing you. Because of this, in circular knitting, stockinette stitch is continuous knitting rather than alternating knit and purl rows. Similarly, for garter stitch in the round, you will alternate between knit and purl rows instead of knitting every row (or purling every row) as you would in flat knitting.

Knitting in the Round on Double-Pointed Needles

Unlike their straight cousins, double-pointed needles, as their name suggests, have points at both ends. Double-pointed needles are generally called for when working smaller items such as socks, mittens, or gloves. The stitches are divided evenly over three, or sometimes four, needles and the remaining needle is used to work the stitches. Double-pointed needles usually come in sets of four or five needles and in lengths of 7 or 10 inches.

It will feel awkward at first to manipulate this triangle (or square) of needles, but as with all awkwardness, it will diminish in time.

1. Cast on 24 stitches on one of the double-pointed needles using either the cable or long-tail method (see pages 12–17).

TIP» Position the stitches in the middle of each needle. Move them to the tip of the needle only as you are ready to knit them. This will prevent stitches from slipping off the ends of the needles.

2. Divide the stitches evenly among the three needles by sliding the first 8 stitches off the cast-on needle onto one of the double-pointed needles.

3. Slide the next 8 stitches onto another needle. Start at the back of the needle (the end opposite the working yarn).

24 stitches divided among 3 double-pointed needles

95

4. Hold the needles in a triangle shape, turning all the loops toward the inside of the triangle.

5. Use the empty fourth needle to knit into the first cast-on stitch on the left needle (Needle 1).

Tips

>> Make sure that the cast-on stitches are not twisted on the needles. Turn all the loops so they face to the inside of the triangle. Be extremely careful that they do not twist—especially between the needles. At the end of your first round of knitting, go back and trace the loops of the stitches with your finger to ensure that none are twisted. If they are, you will need to remove the stitches and start again.

>> As with knitting on a circular needle, when knitting on double-pointed needles, the right side of the work is always facing you. This means that stockinette stitch is created by continuous knitting rather than alternating knit and purl rows.

6. Slide the stitches off the left needle as you knit them. Don't be distracted by the dangling tail of yarn; trim it if it is longer than 3 inches and pull it down and out of the way of the working yarn.

7. Knit the 8 stitches on Needle 1, then rotate the triangle and start knitting into the first stitch on Needle 2. Try to pull the working yarn snug to the needle as you make the transition between the two needles in order to avoid gaps between them.

8. Proceed to knit the 8 stitches on Needle 3. When you finish knitting these stitches and reach the marker, you have completed one round of knitting.

I-Cord

A popular trimming for more whimsical projects (such as the Beaver Meadows Felted Purse on page 142), an I-cord is a small, seamless tube that you can knit on a pair of double-pointed needles.

"I-cord" is a name first coined by knitting pioneer Elizabeth Zimmerman to describe easy-to-knit, decorative cording that has a multitude of uses in knitting projects. According to her daughter, Meg Swansen, the original technique was actually called "idiot cord," but Zimmerman "thought the name rather rude" and shortened it to "I-cord." See Zimmerman's classic book, *Knitting Workshop* for many more creative applications for I-cord.

I-cords are incredibly easy to make:

1. Cast on 3, 4, 5, or even 6 stitches (depending on how wide you want your I-cord to be) using the cable method (see pages 76–78) on double-pointed needles.

2. Knit across the first row but do not turn.

3. Slide the stitches to the opposite end of the needle.

4. Knit the next row as usual, from right to left. Pull the working yarn taut against the needle to avoid any gaps.

5. Repeat Steps 2–4 until your I-cord reaches the desired length.

Provisional Cast-On

A provisional cast-on is a method that makes use of a length of waste yarn to hold live stitches. The waste yarn is later removed and the live stitches are picked up and knit in the opposite direction. This method has a number of applications—creating a piece that is closed at both ends (such as a toy), hems, or, in this case, a waistband.

1. Using a crochet hook and a length of lightweight yarn, chain 20 stitches.

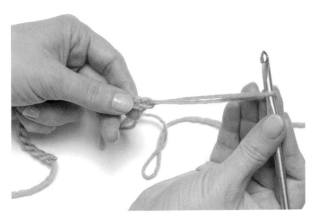

2. When you reach the end of the chain, slip the last stitch off the crochet hook and pull the loop out long to make it easy to find.

3. Cut the yarn, leaving a 5-inch tail.

4. Turn the chain over to the back side, with the bumps visible.

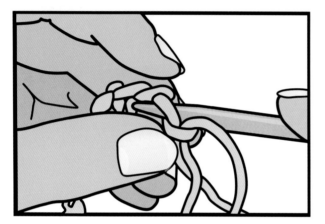

5. Insert the needle into the bump on the back side of the chain as if to purl, inserting the needle from the top to the bottom of the bump.

6. Loop the project yarn (blue, here) over the needle and pull it through, picking up a stitch.

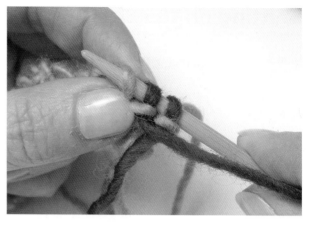

The needle with two picked-up stitches, starting to pick up the third

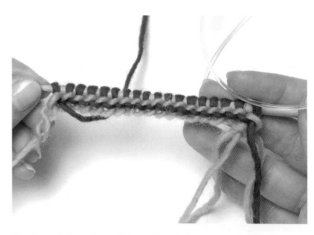

7. Repeat Step 5 to pick up 18 stitches.

> **TIP»** Always chain 2 more stitches than you need to cast on. (For example, for the Sugar Run Skirt on page 135, you will chain 200 stitches to pick up the 198 required for the cast-on.)

To use the stitches later, carefully unravel the chain one stitch at a time, picking up each loop on your needle as it is released from the chain. Knit in these loops as indicated in the pattern.

Knitting on the Bias

Knitting on the bias, also called diagonal knitting, is a valuable technique that can be applied to any stitch pattern. It can be used to create unusual style lines or to create an unconventional drape of a standard garment. The Heart's Content Scarf (page 116), for example, benefits from the diagonal, which adds some flair to the basic straight up-and-down scarf pattern. Bias knitting is achieved by working increases and matching decreases at either side of the garment. While the increase pushes the garment out in one direction, the decrease on the other side pulls it back in the opposite direction. The effect is a garment that grows on a slant rather than straight up and down.

You can experiment with knitting on the bias by knitting swatches that slant in opposite directions.

Bias Left Swatch

1. Using some scrap yarn (preferably a worsted weight), cast on 20 stitches. Work 4 rows of garter stitch.

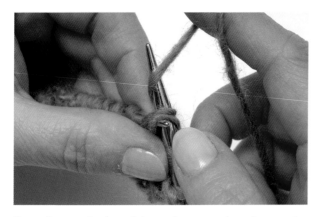

2. In the next (right-side) row, knit 2 stitches, then work an ssk decrease.

3. Knit 14 stitches, then work an M1 increase.

4. Knit 2 stitches to finish the row.

5. On the next (wrong-side) row, k2, p16, k2.

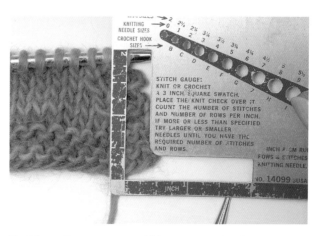

6. After a few rows, you will begin to notice that your swatch is starting to slant diagonally to the left.

7. Work Rows 1 and 2 for a total of 20 rows, then work 4 rows of garter stitch. Bind off loosely in knit.

Bias Right Swatch

1. Cast on 20 stitches. Work 4 rows of garter stitch.

2. In the next (right-side) row, knit 2 stitches, then work an M1 increase.

3. Knit 14 stitches, then work a k2tog decrease.

4. Knit 2 stitches to finish the row.

5. On the next (wrong-side) row, k2, p16, k2.

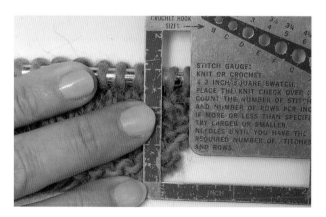

6. After a few rows, you will begin to notice that your swatch is starting to slant diagonally to the right.

7. Work Rows 1 and 2 for a total of 20 rows, then work 4 rows of garter stitch. Bind off loosely in knit.

Looking at the finished swatches side by side shows the effect of biasing.

Picking Up Stitches

When joining pieces of a garment together, it is often possible to avoid having to sew them together later by knitting them together as you go, using a technique by which stitches are "picked up" from the edge of the piece that is to be joined. This technique eliminates the bulky seam that comes from joining a garment by sewing and is used most commonly on neckbands, armholes, heels of socks, and thumbs of mittens.

Tips

» Knitting patterns often use "pick up" and "pick up and knit" interchangeably. Regardless of what the pattern calls it, you are doing the same thing—pulling up a loop through the edge of the fabric (as if you were knitting through the edge). Once you have the loop on your needle, you do not need to knit it again.

» If you are picking up many stitches along a long edge (when joining a side seam, for example), first lay the piece on a flat surface and use pins or stitch markers to divide the edge to be joined into equal sections of 2–3 inches. Then determine how many stitches you need to pick up in each marked section by dividing the total number of stitches required by the number of sections. Spread this number of stitches evenly across the section. This will ensure that the stitches to be picked up are distributed evenly over the length of the edge.

2. Make a loop with the new yarn and slip it over the needle.

3. Pull this loop through as you would for a regular knit stitch.

To pick up stitches along the edge of a piece of knitting:

1. With the right side of the piece facing you, start at the right edge of the piece and insert the needle under the first stitch.

The new stitch on the right needle is the first picked-up stitch.

Repeating Step 3

4. Repeat Steps 2–3 along the length of the piece, picking up the evenly distributed number of stitches between each marker.

A row of picked-up stitches

The second picked-up stitch

TIP» After you pick up all the stitches across the edge on the right needle, you will be at the end of the right side of the garment (the far left edge). If you are knitting in a pattern, you will need to return to the right side of the garment to start the pattern by turning the work to the wrong side and purling a row. Once you turn the work back to the right side you can start working your pattern.

Alternate Ways of Binding Off

On page 53 you learned a basic bind-off. For most projects, this is the bind-off method you'll use. But there are other ways to bind off a project, and sometimes one of these methods will be better. Another finishing method, the Kitchener stitch (not technically a bind-off, but still a way to get the live stitches securely off your needles), is used primarily for the toes of socks.

The Three-Needle Bind-Off

The three-needle bind-off provides the ideal way to join together two identical seams smoothly and evenly. This technique should be used to join the shoulder seams in the Biscayne Bay Shell (page 156). When using this technique, the stitches should still be on the needles (or on a stitch holder) and each needle must have the same number of stitches as the other one.

To join the shoulder seams together using this technique:

1. Place the two right sides of the garment together, with the stitches to be joined still on the needles and the stitch holder. Hold the needle and the holder parallel.

> **TIP»** Make sure to use a large stitch holder so you will have plenty of room to knit from it.

2. Insert a third needle into the first two stitches on both needles, as if to knit.

3. Knit the two stitches together. You should have one stitch on the right needle.

4. Repeat Step 2 with the next set of stitches, knitting them together as one. You will now have two stitches on the right needle.

5. Using the point of the left needle, lift the first knit stitch up and pass it over the second stitch.

6. Slide the stitch off the right needle.

7. Knit the next set of two stitches and repeat Steps 5–6 to bind off the next set of stitches on the right needle.

8. Continue binding off until you are left with only one stitch on your right needle.

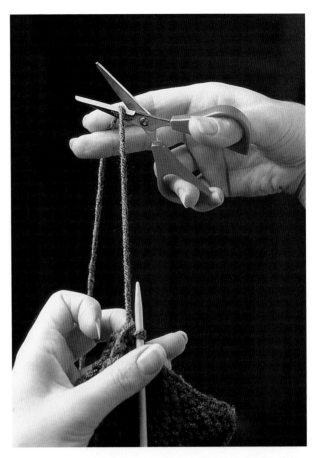

9. Cut the working yarn, leaving a 3-inch tail, and pull the cut end through the final stitch to finish off.

The shoulder seam from the right side of the garment

Twice-Worked Bind-Off

Some projects (such as the Lantz Corners shawl on page 174) require a special bind-off in order to make sure that the edge does not pull or pucker. Master knitter Judy Pascale developed this special "twice-worked bind-off" technique. It provides abundant elasticity.

1. Cast on 20 stitches and work a 20-row swatch in stockinette. Then work 4 rows of a garter stitch border.

2. Purl the first 2 stitches of the next round, then bind off the first stitch.

3. Return the stitch on the right-hand needle to the left-hand needle.

4. Purl these 2 stitches together.

5. Now purl a second stitch.

6. Bind off the first stitch on the needle.

7. Repeat from Step 3, and continue until all stitches are bound off.

The finished bound-off edge shows the elasticity that this bind-off method produces.

Kitchener Stitch

Kitchener stitch, also known as "grafting," is a method for joining together two sets of live stitches in a smooth, tight seam. The technique is named after Lord Kitchener, who during World War I contributed a sock pattern with a grafted toe for women in the United States and Canada to knit for the soldiers in the trenches. Kitchener stitch is most commonly used for the toe seams of socks, but you may also use it in other situations, such as for underarm seams in sweaters constructed from the bottom up (such as the Bottom-Up Cardigan on page 168).

1. Begin by arranging the stitches to be grafted together on two needles, with the same number of stitches on each needle. Hold the needles parallel, with the wrong sides of the knitting facing one another.

2. Cut the working yarn, leaving an ample tail (at least twice the length of the stitches on the needles). Thread the tail through the eye of a tapestry needle.

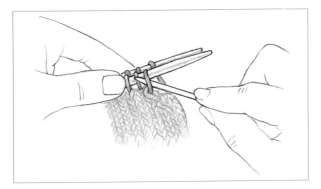

3. Holding the needles in your left hand, with the work pushed to the end of the points facing right, draw the tapestry needle through the first stitch on the front needle as if to purl. Leave it on the needle.

4. Now, draw the needle through the first stitch on the back needle as if to knit. Leave it on the needle.

5. Draw the needle through the first stitch on the front needle as if to knit.

6. Slip the stitch off the needle.

7. Draw the needle through the next stitch on the front needle as if to purl. Leave it on the needle.

8. Carry the working yarn under the needles and draw the needle through the first stitch on the back needle as if to purl.

9. Slip the stitch off the needle.

10. Draw the needle through the next stitch on the back needle as if to knit. Leave it on the needle.

11. Repeat Steps 5–10 until you have used up all the stitches on both needles and you have a complete seam.

12. Once your seam is complete, you will need to tighten it by gently pulling the working thread from the back end of the seam to the front. Use the needle to pull the loose seam stitches tighter. Don't pull too tightly.

A finished Kitchener stitch toe seam

Felting

Felting is a popular finishing method that can completely transform the appearance of a knitted piece. In the felting process, the fibers of the yarn are melded together, creating a thick, solid-looking fabric in which the individual stitches can no longer be seen.

Yarn choice is integral to successful felting; only 100% wool will felt properly, so be sure to purchase the type of yarn recommended in the pattern. Avoid wool yarn labeled as "superwash," which has been treated specially to remove the scales on the fibers that allow them to felt together. Superwash wool yarn is a good choice if you want your project to be machine-washable, but it will not felt.

Felting a piece will shrink it, so projects to be felted must be made somewhat larger than their intended finished size, and you should monitor the process carefully to make sure your project doesn't shrink too much. As intimidating as this may sound, there is a plus side to it—as long as you pay careful attention to what's going on, felting gives you a great deal of control over the exact size and shaping of your project.

To felt a finished knitted piece:

1. Place the finished piece to be felted in an old pillowcase. Knot the end of the pillowcase loosely (or close the zipper if it has one) to keep the piece inside. This will protect your washing machine from excess wool lint.

TIP» Very hot water works best when felting. If your hot-water heater is kept on a lower setting (to save energy or because of small children in your home), you may want to either turn it up temporarily (be sure to warn other members of the household first) or use someone else's washing machine.

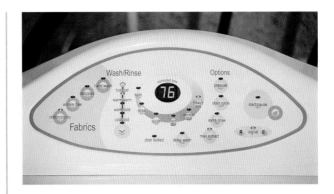

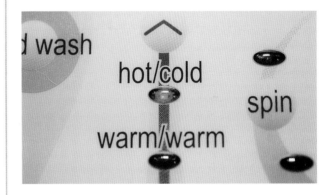

2. Place the pillowcase in the washer.

3. Set the washer to a hot wash/cold rinse, on the cotton/sturdy cycle, and on heavy soil (or any other setting that will lengthen the time of the wash cycle). You only need enough water to submerge the pillowcase, so if your washer has a water level option, set it to the lowest setting. Add a very small amount of laundry detergent and close the lid.

TIP» Washing machines' settings will vary. The two most important are that the water is hot and that the wash cycle is long. You will need to experiment with the settings on your own washer to see which produce the best results.

4. Turn on the washing machine and let it run through the wash cycle. Check on the item after about 5 minutes and every 5 minutes or so after that. Different yarns felt at different rates. Washing machine variations also will affect the total felting time. Checking frequently will prevent the piece from overshrinking. If you are reaching the end of the cycle and the piece is still not the right size, turn the settings for the wash cycle back a few minutes to allow for additional wash time. Do not allow the washer to start the rinse and spin cycle—this can cause too much shrinkage or permanently crease the felt.

5. Once the felted piece has reached the proper size, remove it from the hot water with tongs or a wooden spoon. Remove it from the pillowcase, and rinse it well in cool water. Press the water out of it with a large towel. Do not wring it. For some pieces such as hats, blocking will be required to set the piece in its final shape as it dries. Your pattern will give more detailed instructions on blocking techniques.

Felting in a Sink or Bathtub

An old-fashioned but more labor-intensive felting method is felting by hand. You can do this in a sink or bathtub or any place where you can splash around with a bucket of hot water for a while. You will need a bucket and a new toilet plunger or another sturdy stirring tool.

Fill the bucket partly full with very hot water. Add a very small amount of laundry detergent and put in the project to be felted. If you have more than one project to be felted, you can throw them all in at once; when felting just one project, it can be helpful to add a few other garments or a washcloth or two, to give the project something else to rub against.

With the toilet plunger or whatever other tool you are using, begin vigorously stirring (or plunging or scrubbing) the contents of the bucket. Keep this up for about 5 minutes, then check on the project to see how the felting is coming along. Some people switch between hot and cold water when felting by hand, while others stick with hot alone; experiment and see what works best for you. Agitate the contents of the bucket for another 5 minutes, then check; repeat again and again until you start to see a change. It may take some time—and since the precursor to felting is the wool fibers relaxing and getting bigger, it may seem like you're making the opposite of progress. But keep at it!

Once the project starts to felt, the process moves very quickly, so once you see the fibers starting to meld together, stop to check more often (your arms may be ready for it at this point) to make sure you don't felt it too much. When the piece is felted to your satisfaction, remove it from the bucket, rinse out the soap, and finish as in Step 5 of the machine-felting instructions.

PART II

Projects

Gillian Cowl

This simple cowl is a great project for a beginning knitter. Not only is the stitch pattern simple enough to learn quickly, but it produces a very defined, geometric pattern, making it easy to tell where each stitch goes (and making it easier to tell when you're off). The super bulky yarn makes the project quick to knit up.

SKILL LEVEL

BEGINNER

YARN

Bulky roving yarn, 120 yd (110 m)/3.5 oz (100 g) per skein, 2 skeins
Sample knit in Bernat Roving Yarn (80% acrylic, 20% wool)

NEEDLES

U.S. size 10 (6 mm) straight knitting needles

NOTIONS

Yarn needle

FINISHED MEASUREMENTS

Width: 6.5" (16.5 cm)
Full loop: 48" (122 cm)

GAUGE

Gauge is flexible for this project

Skills used in this project

- The basics (pp. 2–64)
- Knitting through the back loops (p. 27)

PATTERN

CO 25 sts.

Row 1: K1, p1, k1 tbl, *p1, k2, p1, k1 tbl; rep from * to last 2 sts, p1, k1.

Row 2: K1, p2, *k1, p2, k1, p1; rep from * to last 2 sts, p1, k1.

Row 3: K1, p1, k1 tbl, *p4, k1tbl; rep from * to last 2 sts, p1, k1.

Row 4: K1, p2, *k4, p1; rep from * to last 2 sts, p1, k1.

Repeat these 4 rows until piece measures 48" (122 cm) or desired length, ending with a row 4. Bind off.

Finishing

Sew top and bottom edges together to form a loop. If desired, you can add a double twist in the cowl, or you can make it without a twist (as shown here). Weave in ends.

Heart's Content Scarf

At first glance you might think that this scarf requires complicated shaping to create its unusual diagonal dimensions; however, it is actually achieved through a very simple technique known as knitting on the bias. This project introduces the technique and offers suggestions on ways it can be applied in creating other garments. The combination of delicate mohair and cellulose fiber produces a rich texture that adds to the beauty of the finished scarf. Combining different yarns is an easy way to add textural and colorful diversity to a project.

SKILL LEVEL

EASY

YARN

Fingering-weight kid mohair yarn, 200 yd (180 m)/1.6 oz (45 g) per skein, 1 skein

Fingering-weight sparkly rayon yarn, 200 yd (180 m)/3.5 oz (100 g) per skein, 1 skein

Sample 1 knit in Feel'n Fuzzy (90% kid mohair, 10% nylon) and Gold Dust (48% rayon, 44% cotton, 6% nylon, 2% mylar)

Sample 2 knit in Feel'n Fuzzy and Ladera (50% rayon, 44% cotton, 6% nylon)

Note: Hold both yarns together throughout project.

Skills used in this project

- The basics (pp. 2–64)
- Knitting with two skeins of yarn (p. 65)
- Yarn over (p. 71)

NEEDLE

U.S. size 10 (6 mm) straight needles or size needed to obtain gauge

NOTIONS

Yarn needle

FINISHED MEASUREMENTS

5" (13 cm) wide; 69" (175 cm) long

GAUGE

14 sts and 20 rows in stockinette st = 4" (10 cm)

PATTERN

CO 21 sts loosely using cable cast-on.
Row 1: k1, ssk, * yo, ssk, k2; rep from * to last 2 sts, yo, k2.

Tip: Until you get into a rhythm with this pattern, it's very easy to forget this last yo. Make sure to count your stitches at the end of Row 1 to make sure you still have 21.

Row 2: Knit.
Repeat rows 1 and 2 until piece measures 69" (175 cm), ending with a Row 2. BO loosely.

Finishing

Weave in ends. Block the scarf if it needs help getting into the shape you want.

Tionesta Lake Throw

Selecting colors and textures of yarn is one of the most creative aspects of knitting. Yarns come in just about every color of the spectrum and range in texture from the most delicate mohairs to the chunkiest wools. Part of the artistry and creativity of knitting is selectively combining colors and textures to the greatest effect. Designed with the simplest of patterns, this throw is the perfect introduction to this kind of designing with yarn. But mastering the skill is subjective: no one choice of colors or textural patterns is more correct than another. Only with practice (and by knitting swatches—see page 64) will you learn which choices produce the finished results that are most pleasing to you.

SKILL LEVEL

■ ■ ☐ ☐
EASY

Skills used in this project

- The basics (pp. 2–64)
- Knitting with two skeins of yarn (p. 65)

YARN

Yarn in a variety of weights and colors, about 3,000 yd (2,740 m) total (yardage needed will vary depending on weights of yarns selected).

Sample knit in

A: Pop (worsted weight, cotton/rayon blend)

B: Cameo (DK weight, 100% rayon) and Helix (worsted weight, 97% cotton, 3% nylon) held together

C: Miss Mohair (bulky weight, 78% mohair, 13% wool, 9% nylon)

D: Miss Mohair (bulky weight, 78% mohair, 13% wool, 9% nylon)

NEEDLES

U.S. size 13 (9 mm) straight needles or 32" circular needle or size needed to obtain gauge

NOTIONS

Yarn needle

MEASUREMENTS

60" by 58" (152 by 147 cm)

GAUGE

20 sts and 28 rows in pattern and color sequence = 7" (18 cm)

Color Sequence

These 24 rows form the color sequence.

Rows 1 and 2: A	**Rows 13 and 14:** B
Rows 3 and 4: B	**Rows 15 and 16:** A
Rows 5 and 6: A	**Rows 17 and 18:** B
Rows 7 and 8: B	**Rows 19 and 20:** D
Rows 9 and 10: C	**Rows 21 and 22:** A
Rows 11 and 12: A	**Rows 23 and 24:** B

PATTERN

CO 175 sts.

Row 1: *K5, p5; rep from * to last 5 sts, k5.

Repeat this row in the color sequence indicated below until the throw measures 58" (147 cm) or desired length when slightly stretched. Instead of carrying the yarn up the side of the piece, cut it off each time, leaving a tail of 6 to 8 inches (15 to 20 cm) at the beginning and end of each stripe of yarn. When desired length is reached, BO loosely.

Tip: The throw will be symmetrical if you end with Row 8 of the color sequence.

Finishing

To create fringe, tie the tails of yarn together in pairs to secure them. Trim the ends even if desired.

Bayside Scarf

This simple but lovely project is a good introduction to lace patterns. Since you won't need to worry about shaping or finishing, you will be free to enjoy creating the attractive lace pattern and savor the joy of knitting with a luxuriously soft silk/merino blend yarn.

SKILL LEVEL

EASY

YARN

Lace-weight wool-silk blend yarn, about 500 yd (450 m) each in two colors
Sample knit in Jaggerspun Zephyr (50% merino wool, 50% tussah silk) in Aegean Blue and Blueberry

Note: Hold one strand of A and one strand of B together throughout scarf.

Skills used in this project

- The basics (pp. 2–64)
- Knitting with two skeins of yarn (p. 65)
- Yarn over (p. 71)

NEEDLES

U.S. size 7 (4.5 mm) straight needles or size needed to obtain gauge

NOTIONS

Yarn needle

FINISHED MEASUREMENTS

7.5" (19 cm) wide; 59" (150 cm) long

GAUGE

28 sts and 32 rows = 4" (10 cm)

Note: Gauge is flexible for this project, but the gauge given here will yield a finished scarf with the measurements shown above.

PATTERN

Scarf

CO 55 sts loosely.

Rows 1–4 (Row 1 is RS): Knit.

Rows 5, 7, 9, 11: K4, *[k2tog] twice, [yo, k1] 3 times, yo, [sl1, k1, psso] twice, k1; rep from * to last 3 sts, k3.

Rows 6, 8, 10, 12: K3, purl to last 3 sts, k3.

These 12 rows form pattern.

Work in pattern for 59" (150 cm), ending with Row 4. BO loosely.

Finishing

Weave in ends. Block scarf to open up lace pattern.

McDaisy Tablet or Laptop Sleeve

Dress up your electronic devices and protect them from minor scratches with a quick, easy-to-make knitted sleeve. This pattern has two variations: an easy one that is the same all the way around, and a slightly more challenging one that uses intentionally dropped stitches to create a channel to thread a ribbon or cord through.

The stitch pattern used in this project produces a very stretchy fabric, so the sleeve should fit devices that are fairly close to the sizes given here. If you need a slightly larger or smaller sleeve, you may be able to achieve this just by changing the size of your needles. As always, be sure to check your gauge to be sure the project will come out the size you want.

SKILL LEVEL

EASY

YARN

DK-weight yarn, 150 yd (140 m) [240 yd (220 m)]

Small sample knitted in Manos Del Uruguay Silk Blend Yarn (70% merino, 30% silk)

Large sample knitted in Cascade Ultra Pima (100% pima cotton)

Skills used in this project

- The basics (pp. 2–64)
- Working in the round on double-pointed needles (p. 95)
- I-cord (p. 97)

Special Stitches

Dr 1 = drop that single st.

Rt (right twist) = K2tog; leave sts on left-hand needle and k first st again.

NEEDLES

U.S. size 7 (4.5 mm) double-pointed needles or size needed to obtain gauge

NOTIONS

Three stitch markers
Yarn needle
About 1 yard of ribbon ⅝" wide (optional)
Fabric for lining: about 12 by 18 inches [about 17 by 23 inches]

FINISHED MEASUREMENTS

Small (tablet) size: 6.5" by 9.5" (17 by 24 cm) unstretched; stretches to fit a tablet 7.5" by 9" (19 by 24 cm)
Large (15-inch laptop) size: 8" by 17" (20 by 43 cm) unstretched; stretches to fits a laptop 10.5" by 15" (26 by 38 cm)

The pattern instructions are written for the small size; instructions for large size are given in brackets.

GAUGE

13 sts and 24 rows in pattern = 4" (10 cm) (slightly stretched)

PATTERN

Version 1

CO 60 [78] sts (or a multiple of 6). Join to work in the round, being careful not to twist sts. Pm at the beginning of the round.

Rnds 1-8: *K1, p1; rep from * around.

Rnd 9: *Rt, k1; rep from * around.

Rnd 10 and all even rnds: Knit.

Rnd 11: *K1, Rt; rep from * around.

Rep last four rnds (rnds 9–12) 15 [27] times or until sleeve measures 11 inches (28 cm) [16.5 inches (42 cm)] long. Work rnds 9–10 one more time.

Last rnd: Knit.

Remove stitch marker and turn sleeve inside out, with RS facing inwards. Bind off using the three-needle bind-off.

Weave in ends.

NOTE » If you are adapting this pattern to fit a different-sized device, make the sleeve an inch or two longer than the device to make up for the length lost in the bottom seam. Note also that the sleeve loses some length when it's stretched out widthwise, so try it on around the device instead of just laying it on top.

Version 2

CO 60 [72] sts (or a multiple of 12). Join to work in the round, being careful not to twist sts. Pm at the beginning of the round.

Note: A multiple of 12 sts is a big leap. If you need to adjust the pattern a bit to fit your device, you can make smaller adjustments by using a different needle size.

Rnds 1-8: *K1, p1; rep from * around.
Rnd 9: (Rt, k1) 5 [6] times, M1, (Rt, k1) 10 [12] times, M1, (Rt, k1) 5 [6] times.
Rnd 10 and all even rnds: Knit.
Rnd 11: (K1, Rt) 5 [6] times, k1, (k1, Rt) 10 [12] times, k1, (k1, Rt) 5 [6] times.
Rnd 13 : (Rt, k1) 5 [6] times, k1, (Rt, k1) 10 [12] times, k1, (Rt, k1) 5 [6] times.
Rep last four rnds (rnds 11–14) 15 [27] times or until required length has been reached.
Next rnd: K15 [18], drop next st, k30 [36], drop next st, k to end.
Last rnd: Knit.
Pull out the dropped sts all the way down the piece to create a vertical column with horizontal strands of yarn.
Finish as for version 1.

Cast on 4 sts on one of the double-pointed needles and knit an I-cord about 36 inches (90 cm) long and weave it through the horizontal strands left by the dropped sts. Alternatively, you can use a length of ⅝-inch ribbon or a strip made from the lining fabric. Tie the tie in a bow at the top to close the sleeve.

Lining (optional)

1. Cut two pieces of fabric a little larger than the desired finished lining measurements. For the small sleeve, cut two pieces 8¾ by 11¼ inches (22 by 28½ cm), and for the large sleeve, cut pieces 11¼ by 16 inches (28½ by 40 cm).
2. Place the two pieces together with right sides together and sew along the two long sides and one short side, leaving a ⅜-inch (1 cm) seam allowance. Zigzag stitch all the way around the edge of the project.
3. Fold the top edge over to the wrong side all the way around by the length of the ribbing plus ¾ inch. Iron the fold, then sew around the bottom edge of the folded-over part, ⅜ inch (1 cm) from the raw edge of the fabric.
4. Slip the lining inside the knitted sleeve, with a bit of the top edge extending beyond the edge of the knitting. Sew the lining to the sleeve by hand along the line from sewing the top edge seam.

Adirondack Mittens

This simple mitten pattern is designed to give you lots of options. Not only is there a mitten option and a fingerless mitts option, but you can change the size of the finished mittens by varying the weight of the yarn you use. Made with worsted-weight yarn, these mittens will fit an adult with large hands; in DK-weight yarn, they'll fit an adult with small hands (you could take it even farther and try them in sock yarn for a child). Other than the weight of the yarn, the patterns for the two sizes are almost identical; where they vary, the regular text has the information for the small size, and the information for the large size is in square brackets. This pattern is good practice for learning to read patterns with multiple sizes, which includes most garment patterns.

SKILL LEVEL

INTERMEDIATE

Skills used in this project

- The basics (pp. 2–64)
- Working in the round on double-pointed needles (p. 95)
- Picking up stitches (pp. 102)

 YARN

Small: DK-weight yarn, 213 yd (195 m)/3.5 oz (100 g) per skein, 1 skein for mitts, 2 for mittens

Sample knit in Cascade Yarns Pacific (40% superwash merino, 60% acrylic) in Lucky Clover

 YARN

Large: Worsted-weight yarn, 200 yd (180 m)/3.5 oz (100 g) per skein, 1 skein for mitts, 2 for mittens

Sample knit in Plymouth Yarn Encore Tweed (75% acrylic, 22% wool, 3% rayon) in Hunter

NEEDLES

Small: U.S. size 4 (3.5 mm) double-pointed needles or size needed to obtain gauge

Large: U.S. size 6 (4 mm) double-pointed needles or size needed to obtain gauge

NOTIONS

2 stitch markers

Stitch holder or piece of scrap yarn

Yarn needle

FINISHED MEASUREMENTS

Small mitts: 7.5" (19 cm) long

Small mittens: 9.5" (24 cm) long

Large mitts: 8.5" (22 cm) long

Large mittens: 12" (30 cm) long

GAUGE

Small: 12 sts and 15 rows in stockinette st = 2" (5 cm)

Large: 9 sts and 13 rows in stockinette st = 2" (5 cm)

Pattern Notes

The difference between the two sizes of these mittens is due almost entirely to the yarn weight. However, there are a few places where the pattern is slightly different. In these spots, the pattern as written is for the small size; changes for large are given in brackets.

2X1 MISTAKE RIB PATTERN

Rnd 1: *K2, p1; rep from * to end.

Rnd 2: *K2, p1; rep from * to end.

Rnd 3: *K1, p2; rep from * to end.

PATTERN

Cuff

CO 42 sts.

Work mistake rib pattern, repeating the 3 sts of each round around the entire round until cuff measures 2.75 inches (7 cm) (or desired length).

Right Hand

Rnd 1: K6, work mistake rib pattern on next 9 sts, k6, place marker, k2, place marker, k19.

Rnd 2: K6, work mistake rib pattern on next 9 sts, k27.

Rnds 3–6: Rep rnd 2.

Rnd 4: K6, work mistake rib pattern on next 9 sts, k6, inc twice, k19.

Rnd 5: K6, work mistake rib pattern on next 9 sts, k to end.

Rnd 6: Rep rnd 5.

Rnd 7: K6, work mistake rib pattern on next 9 sts, k6, inc, k to last st before 2nd marker, inc, k to end.

Rep rnds 5–7 until there are 14 [16] sts between the markers.

> **NOTE »** You can use any increase method you like for these mittens (except for yarn over, which will leave big gaps). I recommend using a raised increase, which is nearly invisible.

Mitts

Thumb ribbing round: K6, work mistake rib pattern on next 9 sts, k to first marker, work mistake rib pattern to 2nd marker, k to end.

Repeat this round 4 more times.

Bind-off round: K6, work mistake rib pattern on next 9 sts, k to first marker, bind off sts between markers in pattern, k to end.

Cast-on round: K6, work mistake rib pattern on next 9 sts, k to gap, CO 2 sts, k to end.

Work Round 5 three more times.

Hand ribbing: Work the 3 rounds of the mistake rib pattern around the entire hand twice (6 rounds of mistake rib).

Bind off in pattern.

Mittens

Thumb dividing round: K6, work mistake rib pattern on next 9 sts, k to first marker, slip sts between markers to a stitch holder or piece of scrap yarn, CO 2 sts, k to end.

Work Round 5 until entire piece measures 8.5 [11] inches (22 [28] cm), or 1 inch (2.5 cm) less than desired finished length.

Dec round 1: *K1, ssk, k2, ssk, k1, ssk, k1, k2tog, k1, k2tog, k2, k2tog, k1; rep from * around.

Knit 2 rounds even.

Dec round 2: *K1, ssk, k1, ssk, sl1, k2tog, psso, k2tog, k1, k2tog, k1; rep from * around.

Knit 1 round even.

Dec round 3: *Ssk, ssk, k1, k2tog, k2tog; rep from * around.

Cut yarn, leaving a short tail. Use a yarn needle to thread the tail through the rem sts; pull tight, then fasten off.

Thumb

Rnd 1: Pick up and knit 4 sts along top edge of thumb hole, then pick up and knit the sts from the stitch holder or scrap yarn to last st. Slip this st to first needle.

Rnd 2: K2tog (last st of prev round and first of picked-up sts), k2, k2tog, k to end.

Rnd 3: K around.

Rep Round 3 until thumb measures 2 [2.5] inches (5 [6] cm), or 0.5 inch (1.3 cm) less than desired final length.

Dec round 1: *K2tog, k1; rep from * around.

Knit 2 rounds even.

Dec round 2: *K2tog around.

Cut yarn, leaving a short tail. Use a yarn needle to thread the tail through the rem sts; pull tight, then fasten off.

Left Hand

Rnd 1: K19, place marker, k2, place marker, k6, work mistake rib pattern on next 9 sts, k6.

Rnd 2: K27, work mistake rib pattern on next 9 sts, k6.

Rnds 3–6: Rep round 2.

Rnd 4: K19, inc twice, k6, work mistake rib pattern on next 9 sts, k6.

Rnd 5: K to last 15 sts; work mistake rib pattern on next 9 sts, k6.

Rnd 6: Rep round 5.

Rnd 7: K to first marker, inc, k to last st before 2nd marker, inc, k6, work mistake rib pattern on next 9 sts, k to end.

Rep rounds 5–7 until there are 14 [16] sts between the markers.

Mitts

Thumb ribbing round: K to first marker, work mistake rib pattern to 2nd marker, k6, work mistake rib pattern on next 9 sts, k to end.

Repeat this round 4 more times.

Bind-off round: K to first marker, bind off sts between markers in pattern, k6, work mistake rib pattern on next 9 sts, k to end.

Cast-on round: K to first marker, CO 2 sts, k6, work mistake rib pattern on next 9 sts, k to end.

Work Round 5 three more times.

Hand ribbing: Work the 3 rounds of the mistake rib pattern around the entire hand twice (6 rounds of mistake rib).

Bind off in pattern.

Mittens

Thumb dividing round: K6, work mistake rib pattern on next 9 sts, k to first marker, slip sts between markers to a stitch holder, CO 2 sts, k to end.

Finish as for right hand.

Work thumb as for right hand.

Finishing

Weave in all ends. If desired, sew buttons to cuffs for decoration.

Universal Kite Shawlette

Knit up a warm triangular shawl with this easy intarsia pattern. The colorwork reminds me of the diamond-shaped kites we flew as children on breezy autumn days.

This single pattern offers endless possibilities. Vary the needle size and yarn to get any style you wish, from fine and dainty to bulky and warm. Experiment with different color combinations. Some variations are provided at the end of the pattern for your inspiration.

The sample is worked using a solid for the main color, with a self-striping yarn for the contrast color. Or do some stash busting and use a different yarn for each stripe. Let your imagination soar like a kite on the wind!

This shawl is worked from the center out, with a ribbed border.

SKILL LEVEL
INTERMEDIATE

YARN
Fingering-weight yarn, 440 yd (400 m)/3.5 oz (100 g) per skein, 2 skeins MC, 1 skein CC
Sample knit in Malabrigo Sock in Cote'd Azure (MC) and Archangel (CC)

Skills used in this project
• The basics (pp. 2–64)
• Intarsia (pp. 89–91)

Special Stitches
M1l: M1 slanting left

M1r: M1 slanting right

NEEDLES
U.S. size 6 (4 mm) straight knitting needles or size needed to obtain desired drape (see gauge info)

NOTIONS
Stitch markers in two colors
Yarn needle

FINISHED MEASUREMENTS
Wingspan: 50" (127 cm)
Center spine: 24" (61 cm)

GAUGE
Gauge is flexible for this project; for a shawl, getting fabric with a suitable drape is more important than hitting an exact size. Knit a test swatch to see if the fabric has enough drape, and if it needs to be looser, move up a needle size or two.

PATTERN
Wind a few yards of MC into a separate ball.
With main ball of MC, CO 5 sts.
Row 1 (WS): K2, p1, k2.
Row 2 (RS): K2, M1l, k1, M1r, k2—7sts.
Row 3: K2, p2, place center stitch marker, p1, k2.
Row 4: K2, M1l, k1, M1r, slm, k1, M1l, k1, M1r, k2—11sts.
Row 5: K2, p1, place intarsia marker, p to 3 sts before end of row, place intarsia marker, p1, k2.
Row 6 (RS): K2, M1l, knit to center stitch marker, M1r, slm, k1, M1l, knit to 2 sts before end of row, M1r, k2 (slip intarsia markers as you come across them)—4 sts increased.
Row 7 (WS): K2, p to two sts before end of row, k2
Repeat rows 6 and 7 until work measures 2 inches (5 cm) in all.

Don't worry if the pattern seems a bit "wonky" after the first few rows; it will take shape as the work grows.

Intarsia Section
First RS row: With MC, k2, M1l, knit to first intarsia marker, remove marker, attach CC, knit with CC to center marker, M1r, slm, k1, M1l, knit to second intarsia marker, remove marker, attach second strand of MC, k with MC to 2 sts before end of row, M1r, k2
First WS row: K2, p to next color change, change to CC, p with CC to next color change, change to MC, p with MC to 2 sts before end of row, k2
RS rows: With MC, k2, M1l, knit to next color change, change to CC, knit with CC to center marker, M1r, slm, k1, M1l, knit to next color change, change to MC, k with MC to 2 sts before end of row, M1r, k2.
WS rows: K2, p to next color change, change to CC, p with CC to next color change, change to MC, p with MC to 2 sts before end of row, k2

Repeat these last two rows for 1.5 inches (4 cm), ending with a WS row.

Break CC and second strand of MC. (Second strand of MC should be on the right edge of the left MC section when looking at the RS)

TIP» To avoid holes at the intarsia corners, lay the yarn tail of the new color over the old yarn, and be careful that it stays inside the loop of the old color when you knit the next row back. You could also wrap the new yarn around the old one and knit the first three stitches holding the yarn tail to the working yarn.

Main Section

Continue working with MC in established increase pattern (rows 6 and 7) for 1.5 inches (4 cm). While working the first row, place intarsia markers at the color change of previous rows.

Work intarsia and main sections 2 more times each.

Final Section

After working the last repeat of main section, ending with a WS row, break yarn. Attach CC and work in established increase pattern for 1.5 inches (4 cm), ending with a WS row. Remove the intarsia markers. Break CC and join MC.

Ribbing

First RS row: Knit with MC in established increase pattern (Row 6) for 1 row.

First WS row: K2, work 2x2 rib (k2, p2; repeat) to one stitch before center stitch marker, p1, slip marker, mirror 2x2 rib (see note) to last 2 sts, k2

RS rows: K2, M1l, continue established 2x2 rib to center stitch marker, M1r, slip marker, k1, M1l, continue established 2x2 rib, M1r, k2

WS rows: K2, work the newly made stitch to fit into the established rib pattern (should be a purl the first two times), continue established 2x2 rib to center stitch marker, work the newly made stitch to fit into rib pattern, slip marker, k1, work the newly made stitch to fit into rib pattern, slip marker, continue established 2x2 rib to last three stitches, work the newly made stitch to fit into rib pattern, k2

Work the ribbing section as long as desired.

Bind off all sts loosely in pattern.

Finishing

Weave in ends. Wet block the work, pinning the corners down, to open up the ribbing so it doesn't pull together.

NOTE » Mirror 2x2 rib: You want the ribbing to look the same on both sides, as shown in the picture at right. Therefore, you can't continue working the 2x2 rib like normal at the spine of your work. When you reach the center, look at the last stitches knitted before the center stitch, and work them in the other direction, reading the stitches on the right side from left to right and working them on the left side from right to left. It's like holding a mirror to your stitches.

The picture at right shows the ribbing on the prototype. The last stitches on the right side were k, k, p so I needed to begin with p, k, k on the left side. Your ribbing might end up different, depending on the number of stitches on your needles.

Variations—The Sky's the Limit!

We are all different, so why should our shawls all look the same? You can individualize this pattern in a number of different ways, using it as the basic template for your own intarsia design. For each of the sketches on this page, the placement of the intarsia markers is the same.

Here are some possible variations for your inspiration:

- Full-sized shawl: For a larger shawl, increase the lengths of the sections. I suggest working each section for at least 2.75 inches (7 cm) for a wing-span of 70 inches (180 cm). Use heavier yarn for a thick, cozy wrap.

- Stashbuster kite! Work each section with a different color.

- Use a different color for the triangles that appear on each side. The whole shawl will be worked in intarsia, using another contrasting color for the triangles outside of the intarsia markers. Alternating the center color will create the striping in the middle.

- No intarsia: Work each stripe the whole length

- Work a few rows of garter stitch instead of the ribbing

- Work fewer rows per section, with more repeats, making narrow stripes

- Progressively increase the number of rows per section, starting with only a few rows, widening the stripes with each repeat.

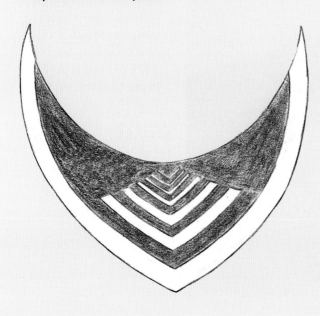

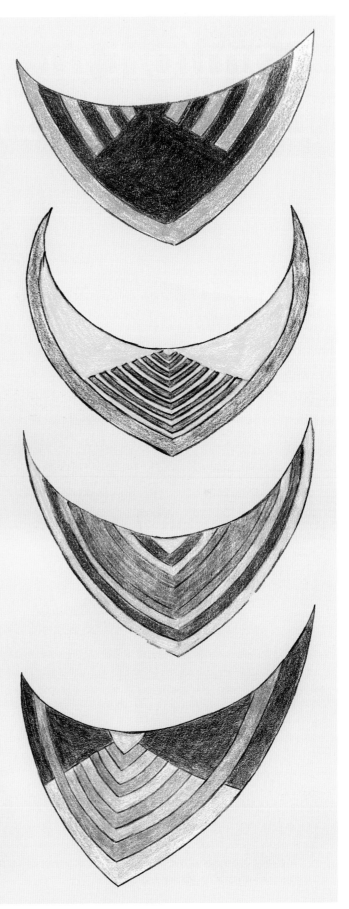

Comfort in Diamonds Throw

Although this huge, cozy afghan may be one of the most time-consuming projects in this book, it is certainly not the most complicated. On the contrary, it is very simple: Once you learn how to knit the basic block, you will simply repeat the block over and over until you have a full blanket, picking up and/or casting on new stitches for each bottom edge and then working each block in the same way from there. Make sure to always pick up stitches from the right side when working with more than one color—there will be small but visible "stitches" on the wrong side of each seam.

SKILL LEVEL

INTERMEDIATE

 YARN

Bulky-weight acrylic yarn, 136 yd (124 m)/3.5 oz (100 g) per skein, 5 skeins each of 4 colors Sample knit in Brava Bulky Yarn (100% premium acrylic) in Peapod (A), Cornflower (B), Solstice (C), and Cream (D)

NEEDLES

U.S. size 11 (8 mm) straight needles or size needed to obtain gauge

NOTIONS

Yarn needle

Skills used in this project

- The basics (pp. 2–64)
- Picking up stitches (p. 102)

Special Stitch

S2KP2: Slip 2 stitches together as if to knit 2 together, knit next stitch, pass 2 slipped stitches over knit stitch.

FINISHED MEASUREMENTS

54" (137 cm) wide; 61" (155 cm) long

GAUGE

1 block = 6.5" by 6.5" (17 by 17 cm) (blocks may begin as squares but will stretch into diamonds as more blocks are added to them)

PATTERN

Block 1 (make 6, separately)

Using long-tail method, CO 35 sts loosely.
Row 1 (WS): k17, p1, k17
Row 2: k16, S2KP2, k16
Row 3: k16, p1, k16
Row 4: Knit to 1 st before center st, S2KP2, knit to end
Row 5: Knit to center st, p1, knit to end
Rows 6–33: Rep Rows 4 and 5
Row 34: S2KP2

TIP» When creating the throw, it helps to think of each block as having a lettered side. Refer to this diagram throughout the pattern.

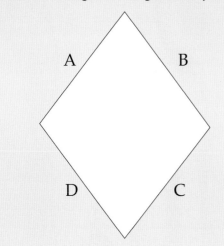

Knitting by Number

You will begin by knitting three Block 1s each in color A and color B. They will form the bottom row of the throw and anchor all the other blocks. From there, you will continue to knit the blocks in numerical sequence (2, 3, 4, 5, 6, etc.) until you complete Block 68. The throw will grow from the lower left corner upwards, with each diagonal row of blocks picking up stitches from the previous row. Be sure to follow the pattern instructions for how individual blocks need to be constructed. Once you have completed Block 68, you will finish the throw by adding the 12 triangles along the edges.

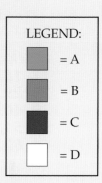

LEGEND:

= A
= B
= C
= D

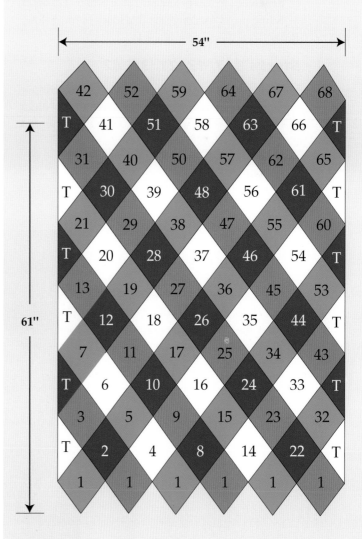

Blocks 2, 4, 8, 14, 22

Following diagram, pu 17 sts along Side B of the corresponding Block 1 in the bottom row; turn work; using cable CO, CO 1 st; turn work; pu 17 sts along Side A of the next Block 1 in bottom row. (For example, when working Block 2, pu 17 sts along Side B of 1st Block 1, CO 1 st, then pu 17 sts along Side A of the 2nd Block 1; when working Block 4, pu 17 sts along Side B of 2nd Block 1, CO 1 st, then pu 17 sts along Side A of 3rd Block 1.)

Rows 1–34: Work as for Block 1.

Blocks 5, 6, 9, 10, 11, 12, 15, 16, 17, 18, 19, 20, 23, 24, 25, 26, 27, 28, 29, 30, 33, 34, 35, 36, 37, 38, 39, 40, 41, 44, 45, 46, 47, 48, 49, 50, 51, 52, 54, 55, 56, 57, 58, 59, 61, 62, 63, 64, 66, 67

Following diagram, pu 17 sts along Side A of corresponding block in row below, pu 1 st in center st of block below, pu 17 sts along Side B of block in row below.

Rows 1–34: Work as for Block 1.

Blocks 3, 7, 13, 21, 31, 42

Following diagram, pu 17 sts along Side A of corresponding block in row below, pu 1 st in center st of block below; turn work; using cable CO, CO 17 sts for Side D of block.

Rows 1–34: Work as for Block 1.

Blocks 32, 43, 53, 60, 65, 68

Following diagram, using long-tail CO, CO 17 sts for Side C of block, pu 1 st in center st of block below, pu 17 sts along Side B of block in row below.

Rows 1–34: Work as for Block 1.

Triangles

Following diagram, work 6 along each side of throw to produce straight edges.

For triangles on left side of throw:

Following diagram, pu 17 sts along Side A of corresponding block below, pu 1 st under center st where two blocks join (placing stitch under will keep continuity of center ridge), pu 17 sts along Side D of block above.

For triangles on right side of throw:

Pu 17 sts along Side B of block below, pu 1 st under center st where two blocks join (placing stitch under will keep continuity of center ridge), pu 17 sts along Side C of block above.

Row 1 (WS): k17, p1, k17

Row 2: ssk, k14, S2KP2, k14, k2tog

Row 3: k15, p1, k15

Row 4: ssk, knit to 1 st before center st, S2KP2, knit to last 2 sts, k2tog

Row 5: Knit to center st, p1, knit to end

Rows 6–15: Rep Rows 4 and 5

Row 16: S2KP2

Finishing

Weave in ends.

Variation

This afghan is equally beautiful knit in a single color—and since you can often move from one block to the next without cutting the yarn, there are fewer ends to weave in!

Sugar Run Skirt

This fun project is knit with a wool-nylon blend yarn, which gives the skirt the elasticity needed to hold its shape. The shifting stitch that carries its way diagonally across the pattern provides a simple but visually interesting decorative element. This project introduces the concept of the provisional cast-on (sometimes called an invisible cast-on), which leaves "live" stitches at the top of the garment to be picked up and knit from the top of the garment up—in this case, to create the casing for the elastic at the waist of the skirt.

SKILL LEVEL

INTERMEDIATE

 YARN

DK-weight wool/nylon blend yarn, 200 yd (180 m) per skein, 4 [5, 6] skeins
Sample knit in Twin Twist (92% wool, 8% nylon)

Note: Yarn choice is extremely important for this project. Look for a yarn that contains a blend of wool and nylon in order to give the skirt the stretchiness it needs. When using hand-dyed yarn, remember to switch between different skeins throughout to maintain color quality. In this pattern, color joins are less noticeable when worked at the C2B.

Skills used in this project

- The basics (pp. 2–64)
- Provisional cast-on (p. 98)
- Working in the round on circular needles (p. 92)
- Cables (p. 76)
- Picking up stitches (p. 102)
- Kitchener stitch (p. 107)

NEEDLES

Size 5 (3.75 mm) 32" or 36" circular needle or size needed to obtain gauge

Spare 32" or 36" circular needle, similar size (for casing)

Size G-6 (4 mm) crochet hook

NOTIONS

Length of lightweight scrap yarn for provisional cast-on

½" elastic, enough to fit snuggly around waist

Stitch markers in 2 colors

Yarn needle

FINISHED MEASUREMENTS

Waist (to sit 1 inch below navel): 33 [36, 39]" (76 [91, 99] cm)

GAUGE

24 sts and 32 rows in stockinette st = 4" (10 cm)

PATTERN

CO 198 [216, 234] sts using provisional cast-on. With crochet hook, chain 200 [218, 236] with scrap yarn. Using main yarn, pick up 198 [216, 234] sts in the chain.

With bumpy side of chain showing, join to work in round (being careful not to twist stitches). Work a foundation round of knit and place markers as follows: *k18, pm; rep from * around. 1st marker must be different to mark beg of round.

First Repeat

Rnd 1: *C2B, k16; rep from * around.
Rnd 2 and each even rnd except Rnd 34: Knit.
Rnd 3: *K1, C2B, k15; rep from * around.
Rnd 5: *K2, C2B, k14; rep from * around.
Rnd 7: *K3, C2B, k13; rep from * around.
Rnd 9: *K4, C2B, k12; rep from * around.
Rnd 11: *K5, M1 (slant left), C2B, k11; rep from * around—209 [228, 247] sts.

Rnd 13: *K7, C2B, k10; rep from * around.
Rnd 15: *K8, C2B, k9; rep from * around.
Rnd 17: *K9, C2B, k8; rep from * around.
Rnd 19: *K10, C2B, k7; rep from * around.
Rnd 21: *K11, C2B, k6; rep from * around.
Rnd 23: *K12, C2B, k5; rep from * around.
Rnd 25: *K13, C2B, k4; rep from * around.
Rnd 27: *K14, C2B, k3; rep from * around.
Rnd 29: *K15, C2B, k2; rep from * around.
Rnd 31: *K16, C2B, k1; rep from * around.
Rnd 33: *K17, C2B; rep from * around.
Rnd 34: Knit to within 1 st of beg marker.
Rnd 35: Using last st from Rnd 34 and 1st st from Rnd 35, C2B, moving the marker to between the two sts just switched; *k17, C2B; rep from * around to last 20 sts, C2B, k18.

These 36 rounds form the pattern.

Work 3 more repeats of the pattern, keeping in mind that each time you do a repeat, you increase 1 st between each set of markers (in Round 11). This means that each pattern repeat will have 2 more rounds in it than the last one.

Second Repeat

Work Rnds 1, 3, 5, 7, 9 as in first set, noting that each round will have one additional stitch after the C2B. (e.g. Rnd 1: *C2B, k17; rep from * around.)

Rnd 2 and each even rnd except Rnd 36: Knit.

Rnd 11: *K5, M1, C2B, k12; rep from * around—220 [240, 260] sts.

Work Rnds 13, 15, 17, 19, 21, 23, 25, 27, 29, 31, 33 as in first set, again with each round having an additional stitch after the C2B.

Rnd 35: *K18, C2B; rep from * around.

Rnd 36: Knit to within 1 st of beg marker.

Rnd 37: Using last st from Rnd 36 and 1st st from Rnd 37, C2B, being careful to move the marker to in between the switched sts, *k18, C2B; rep from * around to last 21 sts, C2B, k19.

Third Repeat

Continue in the established pattern—231 [252, 273] sts after Rnd 11. There will be 40 rounds in this repeat.

Fourth Repeat

Continue in the established pattern—242 [264, 286] sts after Rnd 11. There will be 42 rounds in this repeat.

Last (Partial) Repeat

Work an additional 14 rnds in the pattern (253 [276, 299] sts after Rnd 11). Work Rnds 12 and 14 as follows:

Rnd 12: *P8, k1, p14; rep from * around.

Rnd 14: *P9, k1, p13; rep from * around.

BO knitwise.

Casing

PU live sts from provisional CO one at a time as you pull out each chain stitch—198 [216, 234] sts, pm. *K1, inc by knitting into the st below next st, knit next st; rep from * around—297 [324, 351] sts.

For small and large size, work an additional round, increasing 1 st somwhere in round—298 [—, 352] sts.

Casing rnd 1: *K1, sl1 wyif; rep from * around. Leave yarn at the front of the work as you go on to Rnd 2.

Rnd 2: With 2nd skein of yarn, *sl1 wyib, p1; rep from * around. Leave this yarn at the back of the work as you go on to the next round.

Work Rnds 1 and 2 five more times.

Go around now with a spare circular needle (the same size or smaller), placing every other stitch onto the spare needle and keeping the others on the original needle. You should now have two separate layers of knitted fabric for the sides of the casing. Sew the ends of the piece of elastic together and place the elastic in the casing, between the layers of fabric. Graft the front and back of the casing together with Kitchener stitch.

Finishing

Weave in ends. Block skirt if desired.

Twin Lakes Cover-Up and Hat

This adorable child's garment is the perfect choice for days at the beach or pool. Knit from a cotton/rayon blend in an open lacy pattern, the top and hat provide just the right balance of coverage and coolness to be worn over a bathing suit on hot summer days. This project illustrates two useful skills: how to place shaping in a lace pattern and how to add ruffles to a garment. Following completion of the cover-up, moving on to the matching hat will also illustrate how a pattern knit in the flat can be adapted to knitting in the round.

SKILL LEVEL

INTERMEDIATE

YARN

Worsted-weight cotton-rayon
   blend, 200 yd (180 m)
   per skein, 2 [2, 3] skeins
Sample knit in Wool in the
   Woods Rubble (78% cotton,
   20% rayon, 2% nylon)
   in Squirt

NEEDLES

U.S. size 7 (4.5 mm) straight
   needles or size needed
   to obtain gauge

Skills used in this project

- The basics (pp. 2–64)
- Ruffles (p. 79)
- Yarn over (p. 71)
- Shaping with lace (p. 74)
- Three-needle bind-off (p. 104)

NOTIONS

Yarn needle

FINISHED MEASUREMENTS

Cover-up

Chest: 24 [26.5, 29]" (61 [67, 74] cm)
Length: 17.5 [19, 21]" (44 [48, 53] cm)

Hat

Circumference: 16.5 [17.5, 19]" (42 [44, 48] cm)

Note: Make a hat 1½" (3.8 cm) smaller than actual head circumference.

GAUGE

19 sts and 20 rows in pattern = 4" (10 cm)

Note: To knit gauge swatch in pattern, CO 25 sts. K2 on each side of 21-stitch pattern. Measure over 19 sts.

LACE PATTERN

Row 1 (RS), 3, 5, 7: *Yo, sl1, k2tog, psso, yo, k3; rep from * to last 3 sts, yo, sl1, k2tog, psso, yo.
Row 2 and all even rows: Purl.
Row 9, 11, 13, 15: *K3, yo, sl1, k2tog, psso, yo; rep from * to last 3 sts, k3.
These 16 rows form pattern.

Tips

>> Don't just jump into the lace pattern—remember to knit the three edge stitches first.

>> Measure frequently. As you get close to the length you need, it's okay to stop in the middle of the pattern. Just make sure to use a row counter so you can pick up where you left off.

COVER-UP PATTERN

Back

CO 171 (189, 207) sts. K1 row.

> **TIP»** Using stitch markers can help you keep track of lengthy cast-ons. Place markers after each 50 or 75 stitches.

Ruffle

Row 1: Knit
Row 2, 4, 6, 8: K1, purl to last st, k1.
Row 3: [K1, k2tog] to end—114 (126, 138) sts.
Row 5: Knit.
Row 7: [K2tog] to end—57 (63, 69) sts.
Work 4 rows garter st.
Work in lace pattern with 3 garter st edge sts on each side until piece measures 16.5 [18, 20]" (42 [46, 51] cm).

Neck Shaping

Keeping continuity of patt, work 21 [23, 25] sts, place next 15 [17, 19] sts on hold, add another ball of yarn, work last 21 [23, 25] sts. BO 2 sts each neck edge once—19 [21, 23] sts. Work until piece measures 17.5 [19, 21]" (44 [48, 53] cm). Place shoulder sts on hold.

> **TIP»** You can bind off the two neck-edge stitches on the wrong side in purl as you work your way back across, but you need to make sure to keep the tension on the first stitch from the new ball of yarn taut by pulling down on the newly added yarn. Bind off the two neck-edge stitches on the right side of the garment in knit.

Front

Work as for back until piece measures 13.5 [14, 15.5]" (34 [36, 39] cm) (end with a WS row) then work neck shaping (below).

Neck Shaping

On a RS row, work 28 [31, 34] sts, place 1 st on hold, add another ball of yarn, work 28 [31, 34] sts.

Cont in pattern, decreasing 1 st each neck edge every other row 6 [7, 8] times—22 [24, 26] sts each side. Dec 1 st each neck edge every fourth row 3 times—19 [21, 23] sts. Work until piece measures 17.5 [19, 21]" (44 [48, 53] cm).

Make sure your decreases slant to the same side as the neckline: use a right-slanting decrease on the right side of the garment and a left-slanting decrease on the left side.

When placing the decrease one stitch in from the edge of the row, always knit the stitch after the decrease (on the left side) or before the decrease (on the right side). Always count stitches at the end of each side to make sure you have the proper number of stitches. See "Shaping with Lace" on page 74 for further guidance on how to place these neck decreases.

TIP» Make a handwritten chart of which rows you will need to do decreases and the corresponding number of total stitches you should have in that row. Use your row counter to keep track of where you are in the pattern. Cross off each decrease row as you complete it.

Always make decreases on odd-numbered rows in this project; it makes it easier to see the pattern in the lace.

Note: This example chart is for the smallest size.

(1), 2, (3), 4, (5), 6, (7), 8, (9), 10, (11) = 22 sts each side

12, 13, 14, (15), 16, 17, 18, (19), 20, 21, 22, (23), 24 = 19 sts each side

Finishing

Knit shoulder seams together with the three-needle bind-off (see page 104).

Neck Binding

PU and knit 24 (26, 28) sts from left shoulder seam to center st, knit st on hold, PU and knit 24 (26, 28) sts to shoulder seam, PU and knit 4 sts to back holder, knit 15 (17, 19) sts from back holder, PU and knit 4 sts to shoulder seam. PM.

Rnd 1: Purl.

Rnd 2: Knit to within 2 sts of marked center st, ssk, k1, k2tog, knit to end.

Rnd 3: Purl.

BO loosely in knit.

Twisted Cord Closure (make 2)

Make a twisted cord to tie the sides of the cover-up together. Cut two 36-inch (1 m) lengths of the yarn you used for the project and knot them together at both ends. Slip one end around a pencil or over a doorknob and twist the two strands together until the entire length of the yarn is twisted but not puckering. With one finger in the middle of the cord, bring the knotted ends together; the cord will twist up on itself (you can remove your finger from the middle as soon as the twist has been established with the cord folded evenly in half). Knot the knotted ends together to secure the twist. Weave the cord through a yo in the lace pattern on each side and tie in a bow.

Finishing

Weave in ends. Block cover-up to open up lace pattern.

Skills used in this project

- The basics (pp. 2–64)
- Working in the round on circular needles (p. 92)
- Working in the round on double-pointed needles (p. 95)
- Ruffles (p. 79)
- Yarn over (p. 71)
- Shaping with lace (p. 74)

HAT PATTERN

CO 243 (261, 279) sts. PM and join. P1 rnd.

TIP» It may work best to use three different needles to work this hat. Start out with a 24" circular, then change to a 16" circular, and finally to double points.

Ruffle

Rnd 1: Knit.
Rnd 2: Knit.
Rnd 3: [K1, k2tog] to end—162 [174, 186] sts.
Rnd 4: Knit.
Rnd 5: Knit.
Rnd 6: Knit.
Rnd 7: [K2tog] to end—81 [87, 93] sts.
Rnd 8: Knit.
Rnd 9: Knit.
Rnd 10: Purl.
Rnd 11: Knit, decreasing 3 sts evenly around—78 [84, 90] sts.
Rnd 12: Purl.
Work Rnds 1 through 8 of pattern.

NOTE» Work only the part of the lace pattern between the *s, since you are in the round. Work all WS rounds in knit.

Garter Ridge 1

Rnd 1: Knit, decreasing 6 sts evenly around—72 [78, 84] sts.
Rnd 2: Purl.
Work Rnds 9 through 14 [16, 16] of pattern.

Garter Ridge 2

Rnd 1: [K2tog] around—36 [39, 42] sts.
Rnd 2: Purl, decreasing 3 sts evenly around on 17.5" size only—36 [36, 42] sts.
Work Rnds 1 through 4 [6, 8] of pattern.

Finishing

Rnd 1: [K2tog] around—18 [18, 21] sts.
Rnd 2: Purl.
Rnd 3: Knit, decreasing 6 sts evenly around—12 [12, 15] sts.
Rnd 4: Knit.
Rnd 5: Repeat Rnd 3—6 [6, 9] sts.
Rnd 6: Knit.
Cut yarn, leaving an 8-inch (20-cm) tail. Thread tail through a yarn needle. Work the yarn needle through each live st as you remove them from knitting needles. Draw tight and fasten off.
Weave in ends and block hat to open up lace pattern and establish shape.

Beaver Meadows Felted Purse

Felted bags have become increasingly popular in recent years, and with good reason. Knit loosely on large needles and then shrunk down through washing in hot water, these projects can be completed in much less time than it would appear. The floral appliqué work in this project adds an element of whimsy to the traditional felted purse.

SKILL LEVEL

INTERMEDIATE

 YARN

Worsted-weight 100% wool yarn, 200 yd (180 m) per skein, 1 skein each green (A) and blue (B)

Fingering-weight 100% wool yarn, 200 yd (180 m)/2 oz (57 g) per skein, 1 skein each green (C), pink (D), purple (E), and red (F)

Sample knit in Wool in the Woods Star City in Green (A) and Blue (B) and Cherub in Parrot (C), Cotton Candy (D), Raspberry Fizz (E), and Red Red Wine (F)

Note: All yarns used in this project must be 100% wool (and not superwash wool) in order to felt properly.

Skills used in this project

- The basics (pp. 2–64)
- Working in the round on circular needles (p. 92)
- Picking up stitches (p. 102)
- I-cord (p. 97)
- Felting (p. 110)

NEEDLES

U.S. size 11 (8 mm) 24" circular needle or size needed to obtain gauge
U.S. size 8 (5 mm) double-pointed needles
Size K-10½ (6.5 mm) crochet hook

NOTIONS

Yarn needle
6 large yellow buttons for flower centers (JHB #53291 used in sample)
9" by 5" (23 by 13 cm) piece of stiff plastic for bottom of bag

FINISHED MEASUREMENTS

Finished bottom rectangle: 9" by 5" (23 by 13 cm)
Height: 8" (20 cm)

GAUGE

12 sts and 14 rows in stockinette st on size 11 needles = 4" (10 cm)

PATTERN

Bottom of Bag

With A, CO 128 sts on circular needle. Mark 1st, 20th, 65th, and 84th cast-on sts (1st marked st signifies beginning of round). Hold needles with 1st cast-on st in left hand and last cast-on st in right hand. To join rnd, slip last cast-on st from right needle to left needle.

Rnd 1 (dec rnd): *Sl 2 sts tog as if to knit, k1, p2sso, knit to last st before next marked corner; rep from * twice more, sl 2 sts tog as if to knit, k1, p2sso, knit to 1st marked st.

> **TIP»** Even if you leave the markers in the first row, you should be able to easily follow the marked stitches by the ridge created by the decreases.

Rnd 2: *K1, purl to next marked st, rep from * twice more, k1, purl to within 1 st of 1st marked st. (Do not work this last st; it will be slipped along with the first st of the round at the beginning of the next round.)

Repeat these 2 rnds until mitred corners meet. Complete this row, then knit 1 more st so that the sts can be divided evenly. Place first 28 sts on spare needle. With right side facing, BO both sets of 28 sts using 3-needle BO.

Sides

With A, right side facing and beginning with 1st marked st, PU and knit 1 st in corner st, then 45 more, for a total of 46 sts along length of rectangle. PU and knit 18 sts along width of rectangle and continue in this manner around, placing markers in all 4 corner sts—128 sts.

Work 10 rnds St st.

Break off A and join B.

Knit 8 rounds even.

Dec rnd: *Sl 2 sts tog as if to knit, k1, p2sso, knit to last st before next marked corner; rep from * twice more, sl 2 sts tog as if to knit, k1, p2sso, knit to 1st marked st.

Knit 7 rounds even.

Work dec rnd.

Repeat these 8 rounds 2 more times.

Knit 5 rounds even.

Work dec round.

Repeat these 6 rounds once more.

Work 5 more rounds even.

Next rnd: K12, BO next 12 sts, k10, sl 2 sts tog as if to knit, k1, p2sso. K6, sl 2 sts tog as if to knit, k1, p2sso, k10.

At this point, turn the piece and knit back and forth in rows instead of in the round (continue to work in stockinette stitch: in rows, knit on RS, purl on WS). You may want to place the remaining sts on a stitch holder so you don't lose them as you work these rows.

Rows 1–2: BO 6 sts, k to end.

Rows 3–4: BO 4 sts, k to end.

Place 8 sts on stitch holders to be used later for handles.

Join yarn where you left off before and BO center 12 sts, k10, sl 2 sts tog as if to knit, k1, p2sso. K6, sl 2 sts tog as if to knit, k1, p2sso, k10.

Proceed in rows as before, keeping the final 8 sts on the needles to continue for handles.

TIP» Make a handwritten chart of which rows need decreases and the corresponding number of total stitches you should have in these rows. Use your row counter to keep track of where you are in the pattern. Cross off each decrease row as you complete it. Always make decreases on odd-numbered rows in this pattern.

Decrease rows are in parentheses:
1, 2, 3, 4, 5, 6, 7, 8, (9), 10, 11, 12, 13, 14, 15, 16, (17), 18, 19, 20, 21, 22, 23, 24, (25), 26, 27, 28, 29, 30, 31, 32, (33), 34, 35, 36, 37, 38, (39), 40, 41, 42, 43, 44, (45), 46, 47, 48, 49, 50

Handle

After binding off last 4 sts above, k3 more onto right needle and place on hold. Switch to double-pointed needles and work 12 rows of 3-st I-cord (decreasing 1 st on first row to get 3 sts). Set aside without binding off.

Join yarn to rem 4 sts and work 12 rows of 3-st I-cord (decreasing 1 st on first row). Graft the ends of the two I-cords together with Kitchener stitch to form a loop.

With A, cast on 3 sts and work an I-cord for 22 rows. Thread the I-cord through the loop on the purse and bring the ends together. Cut the yarn, leaving an 8-inch tail on the live stitches, and thread the tail through a yarn needle. With an extra needle, pick up (but do not knit) 3 loops on the cast-on end of the I-cord. Use Kitchener stitch to graft these loops together with the live sts of the I-cord to form a ring.

Repeat the above process, alternating between A and B, to form a chain for the handle 7 links long (not counting the anchor loop that is the connection to the purse).

Join B at the other end of the purse, where the remaining 8 sts are, and knit two I-cords as on the first end for the second anchor loop. Thread them through the end of the chain, then graft them together to close the loop.

Edging

With B, work 1 rnd of slip stitch around the opening of the bag, passing the handles on the inside.

Embellishments

The finished bag before felting.

With double-pointed needles, make 3-st I-cords for the flowers, stems, and leaves. Leave a 8" tail of yarn at each end to use in sewing it to the purse.

Make the following I-cords:

Stems: With C, make twenty 30-row I-cords, two 24-row I-cords, and two 20-row I-cords.

Leaves: With C, make twelve 16-row I-cords.

Flowers: Make two 96-row I-cords in each of D, E, and F.

Attach the stems, using the tails to tack them down with 4 evenly placed stitches, threading the yarn through the center of the I-cord between stitches. Place a 30-row green I-cord in the center of each side of the purse, a 24-row I-cord to the left, and a 20-row I-cord to the right.

Next attach the leaves (the green 16-row I-cords). Fold each I-cord in half and sew it onto the purse next to a stem, tacking down both ends and also the tip of each leaf.

Finally, assemble the flowers and then attach them to the purse: Thread a yarn needle with the tail of each flower I-cord and insert the needle through the stem at even intervals all the way across (to catch the bottom of each petal), then pull tight (to gather the center of the flower, leaving the petals sticking out). Sew the flower formed to the purse at the top of a stem. Sew buttons in the centers of the flowers.

Finishing

Weave in all ends.

Felting

Felt the handbag in a washing machine or by hand (see page 110). Shape it and stand it up to dry. Cut a piece of plastic the size of the bottom rectangle and place it in the bottom of the bag for stability.

Tracy Ridge Hat

Cables and bobbles make this hat an instant classic, whether you choose to knit it in a more traditional solid neutral hue or in more vibrant contrasting colors. The interesting texture in the hat is achieved through alternating two separate patterns within each round. The hat is worked from the bottom up and the drawstring closure makes this a quick knit. Although modeled here by a woman, this hat would be an equally stylish accessory for a man.

SKILL LEVEL

INTERMEDIATE

 YARN

Fingering-weight yarn, 231 yd (211 m)/1.75 oz (50 g) per skein, 2 skeins
Sample knit in Knit Picks Palette (100% Peruvian highland wool) in Coriander Heather

Skills used in this project

- The basics (pp. 2–46)
- Working in the round on circular needles (p. 92)
- Working in the round on double-pointed needles (p. 95)
- Cables (p. 76)
- I-cord (p. 97) [toggle variation]

Special Stitches

C4F: Place 2 stitches on cable needle, hold at front of work, knit 2 stitches from left-hand needle, knit 2 stitches from cable needle.

C8F: Place 4 stitches on cable needle, hold at front of work, knit 4 stitches from left-hand needle, knit 4 stitches from cable needle.

NEEDLES

U.S. size 4 (3.5 mm) 16" circular needle and set of double-pointed needles or size needed to obtain gauge

U.S. size 3 (3.25 mm) 16" circular needle or one size smaller than main needles

NOTIONS

Stitch markers
Yarn needle
Toggle (for variation)

FINISHED MEASUREMENTS

Circumference: 20 [22]" (51 [56] cm)

Tip: The rule of thumb is to make hats 1¹/₂" (3.8 cm) smaller than actual head circumference.

GAUGE

40 sts and 56 rows in pattern on size 4 needles = 5" (13 cm)

Note: Gauge swatch is worked over 44 sts, set up as follows: 2 edge sts, 12 sts pattern I, 28 sts pattern II, 2 edge sts. Measure only 40 sts and 56 rows of swatch.

Since the pattern is designed to be knit in the round and your gauge swatch will be knit flat, you'll need to simulate round knitting by carrying the yarn loosely across the back of the swatch rather than turning the swatch and knitting a wrong and right side.

The wrong side of the gauge swatch

PATTERN I

Rnd 1 (RS): Purl.
Rnd 2: *(P1, k1, p1) into next st, k3tog; rep from * to end.
Rnd 3: Purl.
Rnd 4: *K3tog, (p1, k1, p1) into next st; rep from * to end.

PATTERN II

Rnd 1 (RS): *P4, k1, p1, k4, p1, k1; rep from * to last 4 sts, p4.
Rnd 2: *P4, k1, p1, k4, p1, k1; rep from * to last 4 sts, p4.
Rnd 3: *P4, k1, p1, C4F, p1, k1; rep from * to last 4 sts, p4.
Rnd 4: *P4, k1, p1, k4, p1, k1; rep from * to last 4 sts, p4.
Rnd 5: *P4, k1, p1, k4, p1, k1; rep from * to last 4 sts, p4.
Rnd 6: *P4, k1, p1, k4, p1, k1; rep from * to last 4 sts, p4.
Rnd 7: *P4, k1, p1, C4F, p1, k1; rep from * to last 4 sts, p4.
Rnd 8: *P4, k1, p1, k4, p1, k1; rep from * to last 4 sts, p4.
Rnd 9: *P4, k1, p1, k4, p1, k1; rep from * to last 4 sts, p4.
Rnd 10: *P4, k1, p1, k4, p1, k1; rep from * to last 4 sts, p4.
Rnd 11: *P4, k1, p1, C4F, p1, k1; rep from * to last 4 sts, p4.
Rnd 12: *P4, k1, p1, k4, p1, k1; rep from * to last 4 sts, p4.
Rnd 13: *P4, k8; rep from * to last 4 sts, p4.
Rnd 14: *P4, k8; rep from * to last 4 sts, p4.
Rnd 15: *P4, k8; rep from * to last 4 sts, p4.
Rnd 16: *P4, k8; rep from * to last 4 sts, p4.
Rnd 17: *P4, C8F; rep from * to last 4 sts, p4.
Rnd 18: *P4, k8; rep from * to last 4 sts, p4.
Rnd 19: *P4, k8; rep from * to last 4 sts, p4.
Rnd 20: *P4, k8; rep from * to last 4 sts, p4.

PATTERN

With smaller needle, CO 150 [160] sts. PM and join. Work 1 x 1 ribbing until piece measures 3" (8 cm), increasing 10 [16] sts evenly on last round—160 [176] sts.

> **TIP»** Place a marker after each set of 40 [44] stitches to help keep track of the pattern. Make sure the marker at the beginning of the round is a different color.

With larger needle, set up pattern as follows: *Work 12 [16] sts of Pattern I, work 28 sts Pattern II; rep from * around. Continue working rows of each pattern as established until you have completed 2 sets of Pattern II and an additional 4 rnds of Pattern II. (For toggle variation, stop here and go to Variation, page 149; otherwise continue as follows.)

From this point, continue Pattern I as before, but Pattern II becomes the following:

Rnd 1: P4, k1, p1, k4, k2tog, p4, ssk, k4, p1, k1, p4.

Rnd 2 and all even rounds: Purl on purl stitches of prev rnd; knit on knit stitches (this includes decreases from previous round).

Rnd 3: P4, k1, p1, k3, k2tog, p4, ssk, k3, p1, k1, p4.
Rnd 5: P4, k1, p1, k2, k2tog, p4, ssk, k2, p1, k1, p4.
Rnd 7: P4, k1, p1, k1, k2tog, p4, ssk, k1, p1, k1, p4.
Rnd 9: P4, k1, p1, k2tog, p4, ssk, p1, k1, p4.
Rnd 11: P4, k1, k2tog, p4, ssk, k1, p4.
Rnd 13: P4, k2tog, p4, ssk, p4.
Rnd 15: P3, k2tog, p4, ssk, p3.
Rnd 17: P2, k2tog, p4, ssk, p2.
Rnd 19: P1, k2tog, p4, ssk, p1.
Rnd 21: K2tog, place stitch marker, p4, place stitch marker, ssk.
Rnd 22: Knit on knit stitches; purl on purl.

At this point, discontinue Pattern I and work the entire hat in rounds as follows:

Rnd 23: *Purl until one stitch before marker, k2tog, p4, ssk; rep from * around.
Rnd 24: Knit on knit stitches; purl on purl.
Repeat rounds 23–24 until 24 stitches remain.
Next round: [P1, p2tog] around—16 stitches.
Next round: Purl.
Next round: [P2tog] around—8 stitches.
Break yarn and draw through remaining stitches to close.

Toggle Variation

Work rnds 5–12 of Pattern II.

Dec Rnd: *[P2, p2tog] 3 [4] times, p4, [p2tog, p4] 4 times; rep from * around—132 [144] sts.

Purl 4 rnds.

Eyelet Rnd: *P10, yo, p2tog; rep from * around.

Purl 4 rnds.

Inc Rnd: *[P2, inc in next st] 3 [4] times, p4 [inc in next st, p4] 4 times; rep from * around—160 [176] sts.

Set up pattern as previously worked, beginning with Rnd 9 of Pattern II and ending with Rnd 4 of Pattern II for a total of 16 rnds.

Dec Rnd: *[K2, k2tog] 3 [4] times, k4 [k2tog, k4] 4 times; rep from * around—132 [144].

Purl 1 row.

Knit 1 row.

Purl 1 row.

BO.

Tie

With smaller needle, CO 3 sts and work an I-cord measuring 12 inches (30 cm). Do not bind off. Weave free end of cord through eyelets of hat. Weave 3 live sts of I-cord to cast-on edge of I-cord, joining into a circle (see page 97). Thread cord through toggle and tighten.

Finishing

Weave in all ends. Fold up ribbed section.

Big Rock Socks

Sometimes mistakenly referred to as "Fair Isle knitting," (see sidebar on page 81) the technique used in these colorful socks is more accurately known as stranded colorwork, because the strand of second color is carried along the back of the garment. Don't be intimidated by the thought of knitting with two colors at the same time; after a few rows of practicing the technique you will find that your dexterity increases rapidly.

SKILL LEVEL

INTERMEDIATE

 YARN

DK-weight wool yarn, 123 yd
(112 m)/1.75 oz (50 g) per
skein, 2 skein each colors
A and B
Sample knit in Knit Picks City
Tweed DK (55% merino wool,
25% superfine alpaca, 20%
donegal tweed) in Tarantella
(A) and Habanero (B)

Skills used in this project

- The basics (pp. 2–64)
- Working in the round on double-pointed needles (p. 95)
- Stranded colorwork (p. 81)
- Picking up stitches (p. 102)
- Kitchener stitch (p. 107)

NEEDLES

U.S. size 3 (3.25 mm) double-pointed needles or size needed to obtain gauge
U.S. size 5 (3.75 mm) needle of any type

NOTIONS

Yarn needle

FINISHED MEASUREMENTS

Foot length (heel to toe): 10" (25 cm)
Heel to top of sock: 12" (30 cm)

GAUGE

26 sts and 36 rows in stockinette st on size 3 needles = 4" (10 cm)

PATTERN

Leg

With A and larger needle, CO 56 sts. Divide sts onto 3 smaller double-pointed needles with 18, 20, 18 sts, respectively, on each needle. Join and knit 1 row.
Work in 2 x 2 ribbing (k2, p2) for 12 rounds. Knit 2 rnds.
Join B and knit 1 rnd, then purl 1 rnd.
Work pattern I twice, then work Rnd 1 of pattern I once more.
In addition to the written patterns, here is a chart of the three patterns used in the Big Rock Socks (see page 62 for guidance on how to read a chart).
With B, k1 rnd, p1 rnd.
With A, k6 rnds, decreasing 6 sts on 2nd rnd—50 sts.
With B, k1 rnd, p1 rnd.
Work pattern II once.
With B, k1 rnd, p1 rnd.
With A, k6 rnds, decreasing 2 sts on 2nd rnd—48 sts, 16 sts on each needle.
With B, k1 rnd, p1 rnd.
Work pattern III once.
With B, k1 rnd, p1 rnd. Break off B.
With A, k4 rnds.
Continue with Heel.

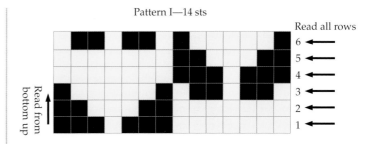

Pattern I—14 sts

Read all rows

Read from bottom up

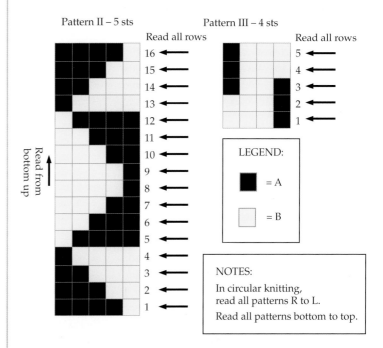

Pattern II – 5 sts · Read all rows

Pattern III – 4 sts · Read all rows

Read from bottom up

LEGEND:

■ = A

□ = B

NOTES:
In circular knitting, read all patterns R to L.
Read all patterns bottom to top.

Pattern I

Rnd 1: *K7B, k3A, k1B, k3A; rep from * around.
Rnd 2: *K7B, k2A, k3B, k2A; rep from * around.
Rnd 3: *K1B, k2A, k1B, k2A, k1B, k1A, k5B, k1A; rep from * around.
Rnd 4: *K3A, k1B, k3A, k7B; rep from * around.
Rnd 5: *K2A, k3B, k2A, k7B; rep from * around.
Rnd 6: *K1A, k5B, k1A, k1B, k2A, k1B, k2A, k1B; rep from * around.

Tips

» When knitting a short section (fewer than 8 rows) of a single color, do not cut the unused color. Carry it along the side of the work.

» Each round has a total of 14 sts between the asterisks. This may help when starting out each round on Needles 1 and 3 (you should have 4 stitches left on Needle 1 when you finish the first repeat and 14 stitches left on Needle 3 when you start the last one).

Pattern II

Rnd 1: *K1B, k4A; rep from * around.
Rnd 2: *K2B, k3A; rep from * around.
Rnd 3: *K3B, k2A; rep from * around.
Rnd 4: *K4B, k1A; rep from * around.
Rnd 5: *K4A, k1B; rep from * around.
Rnd 6: *K3A, k2B; rep from * around.
Rnd 7: *K2A, k3B; rep from * around.
Rnd 8: *K1A, k4B; rep from * around.
Rnd 9: *K1A, k4B; rep from * around.
Rnd 10: *K2A, k3B; rep from * around.
Rnd 11: *K3A, k2B; rep from * around.
Rnd 12: *K4A, k1B; rep from * around.
Rnd 13: *K4B, k1A; rep from * around.
Rnd 14: *K3B, k2A; rep from * around.
Rnd 15: *K2B, k3A; rep from * around.
Rnd 16: *K1B, k4A; rep from * around.

Pattern III

Rnd 1: *K1A, k3B; rep from * around.
Rnd 2: *K1A, k3B; rep from * around.
Rnd 3: *K1A, k2B, k1A; rep from * around.
Rnd 4: *K3B, k1A; rep from * around.
Rnd 5: *K3B, k1A; rep from * around.

Heel

K12 (heel). Place next 24 sts on one needle. Place remaining 12 sts with 1st 12 heel sts.
Row 1: (WS) sl1, purl to end of row.
Row 2: [sl1, k1] to end of row.
Repeat the last two rows until 22 total rows have been completed.

Note: Row 2 creates a reinforced heel.

Turn Heel

Row 1: (WS) P14, p2tog, p1, turn.
Row 2: Sl1, k5, k2tog tbl, k1, turn.
Row 3: Sl1, p6, p2tog, p1, turn.
Row 4: Sl1, k7, k2tog tbl, k1, turn.
Row 5: Sl1, p8, p2tog, p1, turn.
Row 6: Sl1, k9, k2tog tbl, k1, turn.
Row 7: Sl1, p10, p2tog, turn.
Row 8: Sl1, k11, k2tog tbl, k1, turn.
Row 9: Sl1, p12, p2tog.
Row 10: Sl1, k12, k2tog tbl.

Gusset

Setup round (RS): Pick up and k12 sts along right side of heel with extra needle. With another needle, k24 instep sts. With another needle, pick up and k12 sts up other side of heel. Knit 7 sts from heel sts. Place remaining 7 sts on the 1st needle. Needles should contain 19, 24, and 19 sts, respectively.
Knit 1 rnd.
Next rnd: K to last 3 sts on 1st needle, k2tog, k1; knit all 24 sts on 2nd needle; k1, k2togtbl, k to end of rnd on 3rd needle.
Repeat last round until 12 sts remain on 1st and 3rd needles.

Foot

Work in stockinette st until sock measures 3" (8 cm) less than desired finished length.

Toe

Break off A and join B. Knit one round even—48 sts.
Next rnd (dec rnd): Knit to last 3 sts on 1st needle, k2tog, k1; k1, k2tog tbl, k to last 3 sts on 2nd needle, k2tog, k1; k1, k2tog tbl, k to end of rnd on 3rd needle—44 sts.
Knit 3 rnds even.
Work dec rnd—40 sts.
Knit 3 rnds even.
Work dec rnd—36 sts.
Knit 2 rnds even.
Work dec rnd—32 sts.
Knit 2 rnds even.
Work dec rnd—28 sts.
Knit 1 rnd even.
Work dec rnd—24 sts.
Knit 1 rnd even.
Work dec rnd—20 sts.
Work dec rnd—16 sts.
Knit the 4 sts from the 1st needle to 3rd needle—8 sts on each of 2 needles.
Graft the two sets of 8 sts together using Kitchener stitch.

Finishing

Weave in ends.

Teddy Bear Sweater

This is a little project, but it gives you a chance to practice a lot of skills! In making this sweater for a teddy bear or doll, you'll practice garter stitch, stockinette stitch, and reverse stockinette stitch, as well as knitting ribbing and working increases. Constructing a sweater in small scale will give you the skills and confidence you need to tackle a full-size sweater project.

SKILL LEVEL

INTERMEDIATE

YARN

Worsted-weight wool yarn, 100 yd (90 m) each of color A and B

NEEDLES

U.S. size 7 (4.5 mm) straight needles or size needed to obtain gauge

Skills used in this project

- The basics (pp. 2–64)

NOTIONS

Yarn needle

FINISHED MEASUREMENTS

Chest: 12" (30 cm)

GAUGE

20 sts and 24 rows in stockinette st = 4" (10 cm)

Stitch pattern reference

- Garter st = knit every row
- Stockinette st = knit on RS, purl on WS
- Reverse stockinette st = purl on RS, knit on WS
- 1 x 1 rib = [k1, p1] across (reverse on WS)

PATTERN

Back and Front (make 2)

CO 29 sts. Work 4 rows 1 x 1 rib, increasing 2 st across last row (WS)—31 sts.

TIP» Spread the two increases evenly across the last row (Row 4) by working one before the 10th stitch of the row and one before the 20th stitch. You also need to work the increases within the pattern, so make sure that you remember to knit the stitch after the increase. You can use any of the increase methods described on pages 29–40, but a make one (left-slant) paired with a make one (right-slant) creates a balanced row. Make sure to count your stitches at the end of the row to be sure you have 31.

Work 4 rows garter st. Work 4 rows stockinette st. Work 4 rows reverse stockinette st. Work 2 rows stockinette st. Using CC, *k1, sl1; rep from * to last st, k1. Purl 1 row.

Armhole decrease row: K1, k2tog tbl, k to last 3 sts, k2tog, k1.

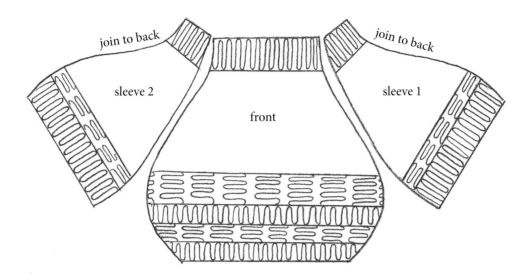

Next row: Purl.

Rep these last 2 rows 6 times.

Using MC, *k1, sl1; rep from * to last st, k1. Purl 1 row (17 sts). Work 4 rows 1 x 1 rib. BO loosely in rib.

Sleeves (make 2)

Using MC, CO 19 sts. Work 4 rows 1 x 1 rib. Work 4 rows garter st. Work 4 rows stockinette st.

Dec row: K1, k2tog tbl, k to last 3 sts, k2tog, k1.

Next row: Purl.

Rep these last 2 rows until 5 sts remain.

Work 2 rows st st. Work 4 rows 1 x 1 rib. BO loosely in rib.

TIP» Since you know you'll be sewing up seams at the end of the project, make sure to leave a longer tail than usual when you cast on for the back and front.

Finishing

Steam block the pieces lightly. Sew the sleeves to the front and back (see tip below). Sew up side seams on body and sleeves. Weave in ends.

TIP» Sew the bulk of the sleeve seam using mattress stitch (shown on page 57), working through the second stitch of each row to leave a 1-stitch seam allowance. The seaming will pull the second stitch on both pieces together, pulling the seam allowance to the inside and forming a neat, invisible seam. When you reach the 1 x 1 rib at the top, catch the horizontal bars at the base of each stitch and pull the two halves of the knit stitch from either side of the seam together to form a whole knit stitch in the rib pattern (leaving only a half-stitch seam allowance). Sew the side seams on the front/back and the arms in the same fashion.

Biscayne Bay Shell

This attractive sleeveless shell is the perfect project on which to perfect your garment-knitting skills. The simple stockinette stitch pattern will allow you to focus your concentration on shaping and finishing. You will also learn how to pick up and knit stitches along an edge and how to sew shoulder seams together from stitches on a holder.

You can work the front and back of this garment on either a straight or a circular needle (see the discussion of straight vs. circular needles on page 6 for more advice on making this decision), but it will be easier to knit back and forth on a circular needle when working the neck and armhole bindings.

SKILL LEVEL

INTERMEDIATE

 YARN

Worsted-weight yarn, 99 yd (90 m)/1.4 oz (40 g) per skein, (3 [4, 4, 4, 4]) skeins of color A, (2 [3, 3, 4, 4]) skeins of color B, and (2 [3, 3, 3, 3]) skeins of color C

Sample knitted in Noro Cash Iroha (40% silk, 30% lamb's wool, 20% cashmere, 10% nylon) in dark pink/#84 (A), light pink/#100 (B), and blue/#104 (C)

NEEDLES

U.S. size 6 (4 mm) straight needles or size needed to obtain gauge

NOTIONS

5 stitch holders (two 6-inch, three 4½-inch)

FINISHED MEASUREMENTS

Bust: 36 [38.5, 41, 44, 46.5]" (91 [98, 104, 112, 118] cm)
Length 21.5 [22.5, 23.5, 24.5, 25.5]" (55 [57, 60, 62, 65] cm)

GAUGE

18 sts and 26 rows in stockinette st = 4" (10 cm)

PATTERN

Back

With A, CO 81 [87, 93, 99, 105] sts. Knit 4 rows. Work stockinette st, beginning on RS, for 3". Knit 2 rows. With B, knit 3 rows. Work in stockinette st, following the stripe pattern below, until piece measures 13 [13.5, 14.5, 15, 16] inches (33 [34, 37, 38, 40] cm).

Stripe Pattern

3 rows color A
5 rows color C
3 rows color A
1 row color C
5 rows color B
1 row color C
5 rows color A
3 rows color B
5 rows color A
3 rows color B
1 row color C
3 rows color B
5 rows color C
1 row color A
5 rows color C
3 rows color B
1 row color A
3 rows color B

Repeat these 56 rows throughout the striped section of the pattern.

Armhole Shaping

Continuing the stripe pattern, work these 21 rows.

Row 1: BO 4 sts; knit to end.
Row 2: BO 4 sts; purl to end.
Row 3: BO 3 sts; knit to end.
Row 4: BO 3 sts; purl to end.
Row 5: BO 2 sts; knit to end.
Row 6: BO 2 sts; purl to end.
Row 7: K1, ssk, k to last 2 sts, k2tog.
Row 8: Purl.
Rep these two rows (7–8) 3 [3, 4, 4, 4] more times.
Work two rows even.
Rep rows 7–8.
Work two rows even.
Rep row 7—51 [57, 61, 67, 73] sts.
Proceed with shaping.

Neck Shaping (Back)

Work even in stockinette st and stripe pattern until piece measures 20.5 [21.5, 22.5, 23.5, 24.5] inches (52 [55, 57, 60, 62] cm), ending after a WS row.

Next row: Work 14 [16, 17, 19, 21] sts, place next 23 [25, 27, 29, 31] sts on a holder, join another ball of yarn, work rem 14 [16, 17, 19, 21] sts. Work the shoulders separately from this point on.

BO 2 sts on the inner edge of each shoulder. (This will be at the beginning of the next row for the right shoulder and at the beginning of the row after the next row for the left shoulder.)

Work each shoulder even in stockinette st until piece measures 21.5 [22.5, 23.5, 24.5, 25.5] inches (53 [57, 60, 62, 65] cm), ending with a RS row. Place shoulder sts on a holder.

TIP» To add another ball of yarn, simply put down the first ball (do not cut the yarn) and start knitting the stitches after the holder with the new ball. Leave a 10- or 12-inch tail for seaming. Work only the 2 sets of 14 (16, 17, 29, 21) stitches on each side of the holder. Leave the 23 (25, 27, 29, 31) stitches on the holder alone. You will pick up these stitches later when you start the neck binding.

Front

Work as for back, up to neck shaping

Neck Shaping (Front)

Work even in stockinette st and stripe pattern until piece measures 18 [19, 19.5, 20.5, 21.5] inches (46 [48, 50, 52, 55] cm), ending after a WS row.

Next row: Work 18 [20, 21, 23, 25] sts, place next 15 [17, 19, 21, 23] sts on a holder, join another ball of yarn, work rem 18 [20, 21, 23, 25] sts.Work the shoulders separately from this point on.

BO 2 sts on the inner edge of each shoulder two times. (This will be at the beginning of the first and third

rows for the left [from WS of piece] shoulder and at the beginning of the second and fourth rows for the right shoulder.)

Left shoulder dec row: Knit to last 2 sts, k2tog.

Right shoulder dec row: Ssk, knit to end.

For each shoulder, work one row even, then work the appropriate dec row again.

Work each shoulder even in stockinette st until piece measures 21.5 [22.5, 23.5, 24.5, 25.5] inches (53 [57, 60, 62, 65] cm), ending with a RS row. Place shoulder sts on a holder.

Use the three-needle bind-off to knit the front and back shoulders together and bind off the work at the same time.

Neck Edging

Using color A and a circular needle and with RS facing, pick up (pu) and knit 18 [18, 20, 20, 20] sts along edge of neck hole between shoulder and front holder, knit the 15 [17, 19, 21, 23] sts from the holder, pu and knit 18 [18, 20, 20, 20] sts between front holder and shoulder seam, pu and knit 5 sts between shoulder and back holder, knit the 23 [25, 27, 29, 31] sts from holder, pu and knit 5 sts between holder and shoulder seam. Place marker for end of round. Purl 1 round. Knit 1 round. Purl 1 round. BO loosely in knit.

Variation

For an easy variation, work the large bottom section and the neck and sleeve edgings in A, and the rest of the shell in a variegated or self-striping yarn.

Armhole Edging

Using color A and a circular needle or set of double-pointed needles and with RS facing, pu and knit 92 [94, 94, 96, 96] sts around armhole opening. Knit 1 round. BO loosely in knit.
Repeat for other armhole.

Finishing

Sew side seams. Weave in ends and block project.

Roxbury Park Cardigan

This cute child's cardigan is just the thing for cool weather. Kids will love the colorful stripes. Knit in one piece from the bottom up, this sweater is seamless with raglan shaping at the sleeves.

The ribbed button band is knitted along with the body of the sweater, so there's virtually no sewing required. The raised stripes are created with garter ridges going around the sweater and a combination of worsted and chunky weights.

SKILL LEVEL

INTERMEDIATE

   YARN

Worsted-weight acrylic yarn, 210 yd (193 m)/3.5 oz (100 g) per skein, 2 [2, 3, 3] skeins of main color (A)

Bulky-weight acrylic yarn, 150 yd (138 m)/3.5 oz (100 g) per skein, 1 skein each of 3 contrasting colors (B, C, and D)

Sample knit in Berroco Comfort (50% nylon, 50% acrylic) 9740 Seedling (A) and Berroco Comfort Chunky (50% nylon, 50% acrylic) 5760 Beetroot (B), 5725 Dutch Teal (C), and 5780 Dried Plum (D)

Skills used in this project
- **The basics (pp. 2–64)**
- **Working in the round on double-pointed needles (p. 95)**
- **Kitchener stitch (p. 107)**

NEEDLES

U.S. size 7 (4.5 mm) straight needles or size needed to obtain gauge

U.S. size 6 (4.0 mm) straight needles or 0.5 mm smaller than main needles

Set of double-pointed needles in same size as main needles for sleeves

NOTIONS

4 [5, 5, 6] buttons, 0.75" [2 cm] in diameter

Stitch markers

Yarn needle

FINISHED MEASUREMENTS

Chest (sweater closed): 23 [26, 28, 30]" (58 [66, 71, 76] cm)

Sleeve length to underarm: 9.5 [11.5, 12.5, 13.5]" (24 [29, 31.5, 34] cm)

Pattern is written for size 2; changes for sizes 4, 6, and 8 are given in brackets.

GAUGE

18 sts and 28 rows in stockinette stitch on size 7 needles = 4" (10 cm)

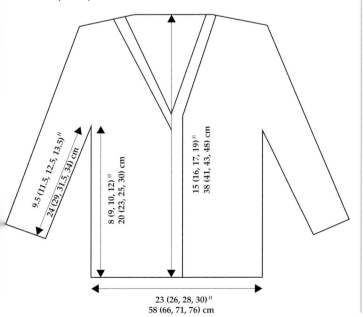

23 (26, 28, 30)"
58 (66, 71, 76) cm

PATTERN

Body

With smaller needles, CO 114 [126, 138, 146] sts in color (A).

Row 1: *K2, p2; repeat from * to end of row, ending with k2. This will be the RS of the cardigan. Mark with a safety pin, open stitch marker, or a bit of scrap yarn to help remember it.

Slip the first st of each row knitwise throughout the pattern.

Continue in k2, p2 ribbing for 1 in. (2.5 cm). Work a buttonhole as follows:

On RS (for girl's style) or WS (for boy's style), work 3 sts in patt, then work a buttonhole as described in the sidebar on page 162.

Continue in rib pattern.

Work second buttonhole after 2 [1.75, 2, 2] in. (5 [4, 5, 5] cm).

Work even in rib pattern for 2 [2.25, 2.5, 2.75] in. (5 [6, 6.5, 7] cm), then switch to larger needles.

RS row: Work 8 sts in rib pattern, k to last 8 sts, work 8 sts in rib pattern.

WS row: Work 8 sts in rib pattern, p to last 8 sts, work 8 sts in rib pattern.

Repeat these 2 rows.

Continue in pattern, working buttonholes as described above every 2 [1.75, 2, 2] in. (5 [4, 5, 5] cm) for a total of 4 [5, 5, 6] buttonholes, and adding stripes as desired.

Stripes

To work a stripe:

Row 1 (WS): Work 8 sts in pattern, join the new color (of chunky yarn), p to last 8 sts. Attach a new ball of yarn of color A. Work last 8 sts in color A.

Row 2 (RS): Work 8 sts in pattern, pick up the chunky yarn and p to last 8 sts. Pick up color A and work last 8 sts in pattern. Cut chunky yarn and weave in ends.

Jogless Stripes

When knitting stripes in the round, you get a "jog" where the stripe color begins and ends. However, there is a way to minimize this effect. Work the first round of each stripe as normal; on the next round, slip the first stitch of the previous round (the first stitch in the stripe color) without knitting it. Continue as normal for the rest of the stripe.

Repeat these two rows for each stripe desired.

To make the stripes as shown, work a stripe of color B after 10 rows, then color C after 8 rows, color D after 6 rows, color C after 6 rows, and color B after 8 rows. You can vary them if you like. Always start on a WS row.

Continue to work the body in St st, adding buttonholes and stripes as specified (or in your own pattern), continuing to slip the first stitch of each row, until body is 8 [9, 10, 12] in. (20 [22.5, 25, 30] cm) long.

Put body of sweater on a stitch holder, or on a piece of scrap yarn.

Sleeves

Using smaller needles, cast on 24 [28, 32, 36] sts and join to work in the round. Place marker to mark the beginning of the round.

Work in k2, p2 rib for 2.5 in. (7.5 cm).

Change to larger needles.

Rnd 1: *Kfb, k5 [6, 7, 8]; rep from * 3 more times—28 [32, 36, 40] sts.

Rnd 2: Knit.

Rnds 3–6: Knit.

Rnd 7 (Increase Rnd): K1, kfb, k to last 2 sts, kfb, k1—30 [34, 38, 42] sts.

Rnds 8–32: Repeat rounds 3–7 five times more—40 [44, 48, 52] sts at end of rnd 32.

Buttonholes

Be sure to work all the stitches tightly.

1. Knit to the point where the buttonhole will be placed. Holding the yarn in front of the work, slip the first stitch to the right needle as if to purl. Move the yarn to the back of the work and leave it there while you slip the next stitch to the right needle as if to purl. Pass the first slipped stitch over the second slipped stitch. Continue in this way until you have bound off the required number of stitches for the buttonhole (4 st for a ¾-in. [2 cm] button). Slip the last stitch you bound off back onto the left needle.

2. Turn your work. Move the yarn to the back of the work. Now cast on (using the cable cast-on), onto the left needle, the same number of stitches that you bound off plus one additional stitch (5 sts in this case).

   Before the last step of the last cast-on stitch, bring the yarn to the front of the work. Pull up the loop for the final cast-on stitch but before placing the loop on the left needle, bring the yarn to the front; it will then rest between two stitches.

3. Turn your work. Slip the first stitch from the left needle to the right needle as if to purl. Pass the last cast-on stitch over the slipped stitch. Pull your yarn tight. Continue knitting the row.

At the same time, work stripes to correspond to the stripes in the sweater body—color B after 10 rounds, color C after 8 rounds, color D after 6 rounds, color C after 6 rounds, and color B after 8 rounds. (Note that Round 1 of the first stripe of color B will be an increase round.)

To work a sleeve stripe, work the following 2 rounds:

Rnd 1: Join the new color (of chunky yarn); knit using stripe color.

Rnd 2: Purl using stripe color.

Cut stripe color and weave in ends. Continue in stockinette st in color A for specified number of rounds (including increase rounds, if any).

Continue in St st with stripes until sleeve measures 9.5 [11.5, 12.5, 13.5] in. (24 [29, 32, 34] cm), including ribbing.

Place sleeve sts on a holder or waste yarn.

Make second sleeve to correspond to first.

Joining Sleeves

On each sleeve, put 8 [9, 10, 11] sts of the underarm (where the markers are) on a stitch holder or waste yarn.

Lay out the body of the sweater flat. Work 26 [29, 31, 33] sts. Place next 8 [9, 10, 11] sts from body on stitch holders, pm, and join live stitches from first sleeve. Pm, work 45 [49, 55, 57] sts of body for back; place next 8 [9, 10, 11] stitches from body on stitch holders, pm, join live stitches from second sleeve. Pm and work remaining 27 [30, 32, 34] sts—162 [178, 194, 206] sts.

Work even for 0.75 inch (2 cm), ending with a WS row.

Note: We will shape the raglan shoulders and at the same time, decrease for the V-neck.

Raglan Shaping

Row 1: On RS, work first 8 sts in pattern, ssk, *work to 2 sts before next marker, k2tog, sm, k1, ssk. Repeat from * 3 more times. Knit to 10 sts from the end, k2tog, work last 8 sts in pattern (10 sts decreased)—152 [168, 184, 196] sts.

Rows 2–4: Work in pattern.

Row 5: Repeat Row 1-142 [158, 174, 186] sts.

Row 6 and all even (WS) rows: Work in pattern.

Row 7: *Work in pattern to 2 sts before marker, k2tog, sm, k1, ssk. Repeat from * 3 more times, work in pattern to end. (8 sts decreased)—134 [150, 166, 178] sts.

Row 9: Repeat Row 1—124 [140, 156, 168] sts.

Repeat Rows 7 to 10 until 18 [22, 26, 30] sts remain between the 2 markers in the back section.

On the next (RS) row, work the front sts, and half the sleeve sts. Put these on a stitch holder or scrap yarn.

Put the other side front sts and half of sleeve on a stitch holder or a piece of scrap yarn. Work 4 rows of stockinette st on the back section that remains on the needle. (This will make the back of the neck higher.) Continue decreasing at the raglan sleeve "seams."

BO the back section.

Attach the yarn on the inside of the right front, and bind off these sts except for 8 sts of the button band/border. Keep these 8 sts on the needle.

Work these 8 sts in rib pattern until the band reaches to the midpoint of the back of the neck. Put these sts on a stitch holder or a piece of scrap yarn.

Repeat this process for the left front.

Use Kitchener stitch to graft the 2 button band ends together.

Sew the edge of the button band border to the neck.

Graft the underarms together using Kitchener stitch, sewing up any openings that remain on either side of the grafting.

Finishing

Weave in all loose yarn ends. Block the sweater. Sew on the buttons opposite the buttonholes.

Bottom-Up Cardigan

This cozy cardigan is knitted nearly seamlessly from the bottom up: You'll start by working the body of the sweater up to the underarms, then set it aside to work the sleeve edgings. Then you'll put the body and sleeve edgings together and finish the top of the sweater on all parts at once. The only seams you'll need to make are the underarm seams, where you'll join the top edge of the body to the bottom edge of the sleeve edging. Three options are given for these seams: grafting (Kitchener stitch), three-needle bind-off, and sewing.

SKILL LEVEL

INTERMEDIATE

YARN

Worsted-weight wool yarn, 140 yd (130 m)/1.75 oz (50 g) per skein, 5 [5, 6, 7, 7, 8, 9] skeins
Sample knitted in Shelter by Brooklyn Tweed (100% wool)

NEEDLES

U.S. size 6 (4 mm) 26" to 32" circular needle or size needed to obtain gauge

U.S. size 6 (4 mm) double-pointed needles or same size as above

U.S. 4 (3.5 mm) 26" circular needle or 0.5 mm smaller than main needles

Skills used in this project

- The basics (pp. 2–64)
- Working in the round on circular needles (p. 92)
- Yarn over (p. 71)
- Kitchener stitch (p. 107) or three-needle bind-off (p. 104)
- Working in the round on double-pointed needles (p. 95)
- Picking up stitches (p. 102)

Special Stitch

Sk2p: Sl 1, k2tog, pass slipped stitch over the k2tog

NOTIONS

Six stitch markers
Waste yarn
Yarn needle
Seven buttons ⅝" (16 mm) in diameter

FINISHED MEASUREMENTS

Chest: 33.25 [35.5, 37.75, 40, 42.25, 44.5, 46.5]" (84 [90, 96, 102, 107, 113, 118] cm)
Body length from underarm to hem: 14.5 [14.5, 14.75, 15, 15.25, 15.5, 15.75]" (37 [37, 37, 38, 39, 39, 40] cm)
Sleeve circumference: 11.5 [12.25, 13.25, 14.25, 15, 16, 16.75]" (29 [31, 34, 36, 38, 41, 43] cm)

Note: Instructions are for size XS, with instructions for S, M, L, 1X, 2X, and 3X in brackets.

GAUGE

18 sts and 26 rows in stockinette st on size 6 needles = 4" (10 cm)
18 sts and 26 rows in lace pattern on size 6 needles = 4" (10 cm)

Tip

- Reverse stockinette stitch = purl on right side of work, knit on wrong side
- Garter stitch worked in the round = knit one round, purl one round.

LACE PATTERN

Row 1 (RS): Knit.
Row 2: *K4, p8, k4. Rep from * to marker.
Row 3: *P3, k2tog, k3, [yo] 2 times, k3, ssk, p3. Rep from * to marker.
Row 4: *K3, p4, purl into front and back of double yo, p4, k3. Rep from * to marker.
Row 5: *P2, k2tog, k3, yo, k2, yo, k3, ssk, p2. Rep from * to marker.
Row 6: *K2, p12, k2. Rep from * to marker.
Row 7: *P1, k2tog, k3, yo, k4, yo, k3, ssk, p1. Rep from * to marker.
Row 8: *K1, p14, k1. Rep from * to marker.
Row 9: *K2tog, k3, yo, k6, yo, k3, ssk. Rep from * to marker.
Row 10: Purl.

PATTERN

Body

With size 6 circular needle and long-tail cast-on, CO 150 [160, 170, 180, 190, 200, 210] sts.
Knit 4 rows.
Set-up Row (RS): P13 [16, 18, 21, 23, 26, 28] sts, pm, work Lace Pattern over next 48 sts, pm, p28 [32, 38, 42, 48, 52, 58] sts, pm, work Lace Pattern over next 48 sts, pm, p13 [16, 18, 21, 23, 26, 28] sts.
Continue as established, working Lace Pattern between markers and reverse stockinette st (purl on RS, knit on WS) until piece measures 14.5 [14.5, 14.75, 15, 15.25, 15.5, 15.75] inches (37 [37, 37, 38, 39, 39, 40] cm) or desired length from cast-on edge. End with a RS row.
Next row [remove markers as you come to them]: K32 [35, 37, 40, 42, 45, 47]. If you want to use grafting or three-needle bind-off for the underarm seam, knit next 10 sts, then slip these sts to waste yarn. To sew the underarm seam, bind off next 10 sts.
Knit to 42 [45, 47, 50, 52, 55, 57] sts before end of row. For grafting or three-needle bind-off, knit next 10 sts, then slip these sts to waste yarn. For sewing, bind off next 10 sts.
Knit to end of row.
Set body aside and work sleeve edging.

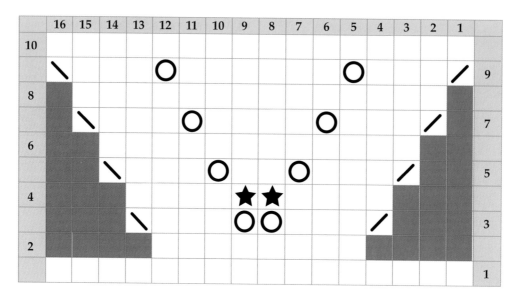

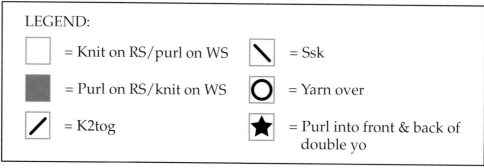

LEGEND:

☐ = Knit on RS/purl on WS

⬛ = Purl on RS/knit on WS

╱ = K2tog

╲ = Ssk

◯ = Yarn over

★ = Purl into front & back of double yo

19 (21.25, 21.75, 22.25, 24.5, 26.5, 27)"
48 (54, 55, 57, 62, 67, 69) cm

11.5 (12.25, 13.25, 14.25, 15, 16, 16.75)"
29 (31, 34, 36, 38, 41, 43) cm

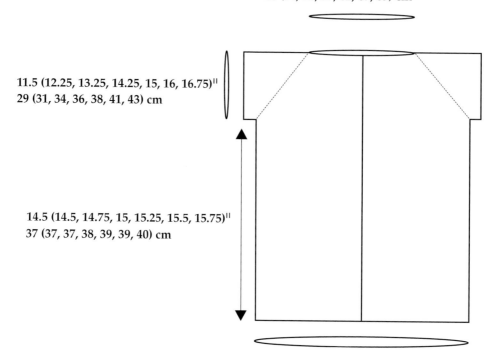

14.5 (14.5, 14.75, 15, 15.25, 15.5, 15.75)"
37 (37, 37, 38, 39, 39, 40) cm

33.25 (35.5, 37.75, 40, 42.25, 44.5, 46.5)"
84 (90, 96, 102, 107, 113, 118) cm

Sleeve Edging (make 2)

With double-pointed needles, CO 52 [56, 60, 64, 68, 72, 76] sts. Distribute sts as evenly as possible and join for working in the round, taking care not to twist sts, and place a marker at the beginning of the round. Work 4 rounds in garter st.

Next rnd: Knit to 5 sts before marker. For grafting or three-needle bind-off, knit next 10 sts, then slip these sts to waste yarn. For sewing, bind off next 10 sts.

Set aside first sleeve edging and work second sleeve edging.

Joining Body and Sleeve Edgings

Next row (RS): With size 6 circular needle, knit 32 [35, 37, 40, 42, 45, 47] front sts, pm, knit 42 [46, 50, 54, 58, 62, 66] sleeve edging sts, pm, knit 66 [70, 76, 80, 86, 90, 96] back sts, pm, knit 42 [46, 50, 54, 58, 62, 66] sleeve edging sts, pm, knit 32 [35, 37, 40, 42, 45, 47] front sts—214 [232, 250, 268, 286, 304, 322] sts on needle.

Purl one row even.

Yoke

Row 1(RS): *Knit to 4 sts before marker, sk2p, yo, k1, sm, k1, yo, sk2p. Rep from * 3 more times. Knit to end of row.

Row 2: Purl.

Work these 2 rows a total of 16 [17, 19, 21, 22, 23, 25] times—86 [96, 98, 100, 110, 120, 122] sts.

Change to smaller circular needle; knit 4 rows. Bind off.

Edging

Left Band: With smaller circular needle and right side facing, beg at top edge and pick up and knit 3 sts over every 4 rows along left edge of front opening. Knit 3 rows. Bind off.

Right Band: With smaller circular needle and right side facing, beg at bottom edge and pick and knit 3 sts over every 4 rows along right edge of front opening.

Place 7 markers for buttonholes: first marker 0.5" (1.3 cm) from top edge, last marker 0.5" (1.3 cm) from bottom edge, and remaining 5 markers spaced evenly between.

Knit one row.

Buttonhole row: *Knit to marker, yo, k2tog. Rep from * 5 more times.

Knit one row.

Bind off.

Finishing

Work underarm seams by grafting, working three-needle bind-off, or sewing the 10 underarm sts together. Close any gaps at edges of underarm seam.

Weave in loose ends.

Block to finished measurements.

Sew buttons to left band, opposite buttonholes.

Bamboo Forest Sweater

This project uses a simple but fascinating technique known as slip-stitch knitting.

When used with just one skein of yarn (either solid or variegated in color) slip-stitch knitting produces a visually interesting basket-weave texture. This technique can also be used to great effect when you add a second skein of yarn in a different color, producing simple color patterns that look like stranded colorwork but only require knitting with one color at a time. Once you perfect the slip-stitch technique with a single yarn color in this sweater, you can then move on to more complex applications with two skeins.

SKILL LEVEL

INTERMEDIATE

4 YARN

Worsted-weight cotton yarn, 200 yd (180 m)/3.5 oz (100 g) per skein, [4 (5, 6)] [7 (8, 8, 9, 10)] skeins

Sample knit in Wool in the Woods Gypsy (100% cotton)

NEEDLES

U.S. size 9 (5.5 mm) straight or circular needles or size needed to obtain gauge

U.S. size 8 (5 mm) circular needles or 0.5 mm smaller than main needles

Skills used in this project

- The basics (pp. 2–64)
- Slip-stitch knitting (p. 69)
- Three-needle bind-off (p. 104)
- Picking up stitches (p. 102)

NOTIONS

5 stitch holders (two 6-inch, three 4½-inch)
Yarn needle

FINISHED MEASUREMENTS

Bust: [28 (33, 36)"] [41.25 (44, 46.5, 49.25, 52)"] [71 (84, 91) cm] [105 (112, 118, 125, 132) cm]
Length: [16.5 (18, 19)"] [20.5 (21, 22, 23, 25)"] [42 (46, 48) cm] [52 (53, 56, 58, 64) cm]

Throughout this pattern, the first set of brackets contains measurements and instructions for children's sizes; the second, for adult sizes.

GAUGE

18 sts and 34 rows in texture pattern on size 9 needles = 4" (10 cm)

TEXTURE PATTERN

Row 1 (RS): *P3, sl1 wyif, k1, sl1 wyif; rep from * to last 3 sts, p3.
Rows 2 and 4: *K3, p3; rep from * to last 3 sts, k3.
Row 3: *P3, k1, sl1 wyif, k1; rep from * to last 3 sts, p3.
Repeat these 4 rows for pattern.

Tips

➤➤ You can only bind off at the beginning of a row. You will have to knit 4 rows to bind off 2 stitches on each armhole edge 2 times.

➤➤ To make sure that your increases slant in the direction of the armhole shaping, do a k2tog tbl or ssk decrease on the right side of the piece and a k2tog decrease on the left side.

PATTERN

Back

With larger needles, CO [69 (75, 81)] [93 (99, 105, 111, 117)] sts. Work 3 x 3 rib for 4 rows. Beg pattern on RS and work until piece measures [9 (10, 10.5)"] [11 (11.5, 12, 13, 14)"] [23 (25, 27) cm] [28 (29, 30, 33, 36) cm].

Armhole Shaping

BO 2 sts at each armhole edge [1 time] [2 times].
Dec 1 st at each armhole edge every other row 4 times—[57 (63, 69)] [77 (83, 89, 95, 101)] sts.
Cont in pattern until piece measures [15.5 (17, 18)"] [19.5 (20, 21, 22, 24)"] [39 (43, 46) cm] [50 (51, 53, 56, 61) cm].

Neck Shaping

Work [19 (21, 23)] [24 (26, 28, 30, 32)] sts, place next [19 (21, 23)] [29 (31, 33, 35, 37)] sts on a holder, add another ball of yarn and work last [19 (21, 23)] [24 (26, 28, 30, 32)] sts.
BO 2 sts on each edge of the neck—[17 (19, 21)] [22 (24, 26, 28, 30)] sts.
Work even in pattern until piece measures [16.5 (18, 19)"] [20.5 (21, 22, 23, 25)"] [42 (46, 48) cm] [52 (53, 56, 58, 64) cm].
Place shoulder sts on holders.

TIP ➤➤ To add another ball of yarn, simply put down the first ball (do not cut the yarn) and start knitting the stitches after the holder with the new ball. Leave a 10- or 12-inch tail for seaming. You will work only the 2 sets of [19 (21, 23)] [24 (26, 28, 30, 32)] stitches on either side of the holder. Leave the [19 (21, 23)] [29 (31, 33, 35, 37)] stitches on the holder alone. You will pick up these stitches later when you work the neck binding.

Front

Work as for back until piece measures [14 (15.25, 16.25)"] [17.5 (18, 18, 19, 21)"] [36 (39, 41) cm] [44 (46, 46, 48, 53) cm].

Neck Shaping

Work [23 (25, 27)] [29 (31, 33, 35, 37)] sts, place next [11 (13, 15)] [19 (21, 23, 25, 27)] sts on a holder, add another ball of yarn and work last [23 (25, 27)] [29 (31, 33, 35, 37)] sts.
Working both sides together with a separate ball of yarn for each side, BO 2 sts on each edge of the neck twice.

Dec 1 st on each edge of the neck every other row [2 times] [3 times]—[17 (19, 21)] [22 (24, 26, 28, 30)] sts.

Work even in pattern until piece measures [16.5 (18, 19)"] [20.5 (21, 22, 23, 25)"] [42 (46, 48) cm] [52 (53, 56, 58, 64) cm].

Sleeves (make 2)

With larger needles, CO [27 (33, 39)] [39] st. Work 3 x 3 rib for 4 rows. Beg pattern and at the same time, keeping continuity of pattern, inc 1 st on each side every 4th row until you have [69 (73, 77)] [77 (77, 77, 77, 79)] sts.

Adult sizes only: Inc 1 st each side every 6th row until you have 85 (85, 85, 85, 89) sts.

Work even in pattern until sleeve measures [14 (15.5, 16.75)"] [17 (17, 18, 18, 19)"] [36 (39, 43) cm] [43 (43, 46, 46, 48) cm].

BO 2 sts on each side [1 time] [2 times].

Dec 1 st on each side every other row 4 times.

BO 5 sts on each side [3 times] [4 times].

BO 6 sts on each side [0 (1, 2) times] [2 times].

BO remaining sts loosely.

Assembly

Use three-needle bind-off to knit tops of shoulders together. Sew ends of sleeves to armholes. Sew up side seams of body and sleeves.

Neck Edging

With smaller needles, pu and knit [14 (14, 15)] [16 (16, 18, 18, 18)] sts along edge of neck hole between left shoulder seam and front stitch holder, knit the [11 (13, 15)] [19 (21, 23, 25, 27)] sts from holder, pu and knit [14 (14, 15)] [16 (16, 18, 18, 18)] sts between holder and shoulder seam, pu and knit 5 sts between shoulder and back holder, knit the [19 (21, 23)] [29 (31, 33, 35, 37)] sts from holder, pu and knit 5 sts between holder and shoulder seam.

Purl 1 round.

BO loosely in knit.

> **TIP»** Be sure to space the picked-up stitches evenly.

Finishing

Weave in ends. Block sweater.

Wintry Mix Hat

This cozy hat is just the thing for a snowy day. Use fingering-weight yarn for a child's hat, and worsted-weight yarn for an adult hat. The colorwork will take some time, but it makes for a warmer hat, since two strands of yarn go around every row. Stranded colorwork doesn't stretch as much as knitting with a single yarn, so be sure to work loosely so that the hat will fit.

SKILL LEVEL

EXPERIENCED

 YARN

Child size: Fingering-weight wool-blend yarn, 200 yd (180 m)/1.75 oz (50 g) per skein, 1 skein each of 3 colors
Child-size sample knit in The Fibre Co. Canopy (50% alpaca, 30% merino, 20% bamboo)
A: Obsidian
B: Orchid
C: Acai

 YARN

Adult size: Worsted-weight wool blend yarn, 98 yd (90 m)/1.75 oz (50 g) per skein, 1 skein each of 3 colors
Adult-size sample knit in The Fibre Co. Organik (70% wool, 15%, alpaca, 15% silk)
A: Crater Lake
B: Arctic Tundra
C: Aquatic Forest

Skills used in this project

- The basics (pp. 2–64)
- Working in the round on circular (p. 92) or double-pointed (p. 95) needles
- Stranded colorwork (p. 81)

NEEDLES

Child size:

U.S. size 4 (3.5 mm) 40" circular needle or double-pointed needles or size needed to obtain gauge

U.S. size 1.5 (2.5 mm) circular needle or .5 to 1 mm smaller than main needles

Adult size:

U.S. size 8 (5 mm) 40" circular needle or double-pointed needles or size needed to obtain gauge

U.S. size 6 (4 mm) circular needle or .5 to 1 mm smaller than main needles

NOTIONS

Stitch marker

Darning needle

FINISHED MEASUREMENTS

Child size circumference: 16.5" (42 cm) unstretched

Adult size circumference: 20" (51 cm) unstretched

Hat will stretch to accommodate a head size 2–3" (5–8 cm) larger.

GAUGE

Child size: 24 sts and 28 rows in stockinette st = 4" (10 cm)

Adult size: 20 sts and 24 rows in stockinette st = 4" (10 cm)

PATTERN

Using smaller needle, A, and long-tail cast-on, *loosely* cast on 100 sts; place marker and join to knit in the round being careful not to twist sts.

Beginning with a purl round, work in garter st for 3 rnds.

With B, knit one rnd.

With A, purl 1 rnd. Knit 1 rnd.

Beginning with Rnd 1, work Chart 1 over all sts. (You will repeat each row of Chart 1 twice around the hat.)

Beginning with Rnd 1, work Chart 2 over all sts. (You will repeat each row of Chart 2 ten times around the hat.)

Beginning with Rnd 1, work Chart 3 over all sts, working decreases as instructed. If using circular needles, switch to double-pointed needles when needed. You will repeat each row of Chart 3 ten times around the hat.

With C, k2tog around. (5 sts)

Cut yarn and thread tail through sts; pull to tighten and close sts, then fasten off.

Finishing

Weave in all ends. Wet block.

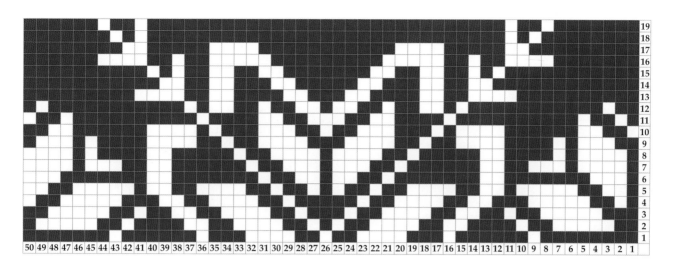

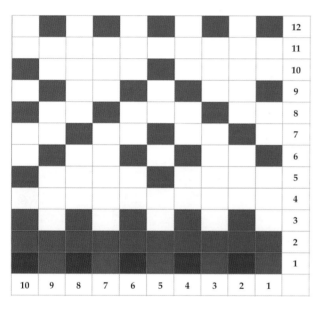

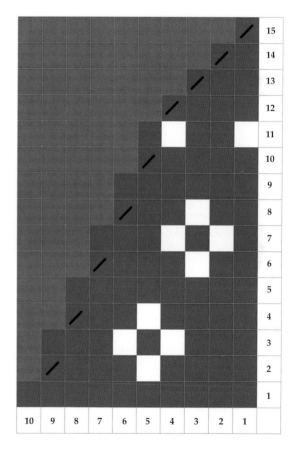

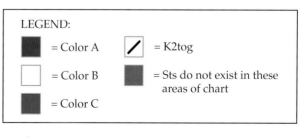

LEGEND:

■ = Color A   ╱ = K2tog

□ = Color B   ■ = Sts do not exist in these
                         areas of chart

■ = Color C

Lantz Corners Shawl

This intricate design starts in the center and works outward, building from just eight cast-on stitches to a final round containing 520 stitches. Its airy beauty is created by a complex lace pattern knit in the round and then bound off using a special technique that allows for abundant elasticity. The cotton blend chosen for the project gives the piece a lightness and flexibility that accentuates the open pattern of the lace. When complete, the square piece can be folded in half, triangle-style, and worn as a shawl or used as a small table cover.

SKILL LEVEL

EXPERIENCED

YARN

DK-weight cotton-blend yarn, 200 yd (180 m)/3.5 oz (100 g) per skein, 5 skeins
Sample knit in Dunluce (57% cotton, 38% rayon, 5% linen) in Natural.

NEEDLES

U.S. size 8 (5 mm) needles or size needed to obtain gauge: a set of double-pointed needles, a 16" circular needle, and a 24" circular needle

Note: Some knitters may prefer a circular needle longer than 24" when working with all stitches to avoid overcrowding of stitches on the needle. Consider opting for a 36" circular, if available.

Skills used in this project

- The basics (pp. 2–64)
- Working in the round on double-pointed needles (p. 95)
- Working in the round on circular needles (p. 92)
- Yarn over (p. 71)
- Twice-worked bind-off (p. 106)

NOTIONS

Stitch markers
Yarn needle

FINISHED MEASUREMENTS

40" by 40" (102 by 102 cm)

GAUGE

15 sts and 21 rows in stockinette st (wet blocked) = 4" (10 cm)

PATTERN

CO 8 sts. Divide sts evenly onto 4 double-pointed needles (2 sts on each needle). PM, join, and knit 1 rnd.

Note: From this point forward all instructions will be repeated around. Each instruction will be worked a total of 4 times around. To calculate number of sts in a rnd, multiply the st number at the end of each instruction by 4.

NOTE» This project is constructed from the center outward, which means you will have to switch from double-pointed needles to a circular needle (and from a smaller circular needle to a longer one) as it grows. It doesn't matter when you make these switches; change to longer needles whenever the stitches are too crowded for you to work with comfortably.

Rnd 1: *Yo, k1, yo, k1; rep from * around—16 sts.
Rnd 2 (and all other even rounds unless otherwise specified): Knit.
Rnd 3: *Yo, k1, yo, ssk, yo, k1; rep from * around—24 sts.
Rnd 5: *Yo, k2tog, yo, k1, yo, ssk, yo, k1; rep from * around—32 sts.
Rnd 7: *Yo, k2, yo, p3tog, yo, k2, yo, k1; rep from * around—40 sts.

Rnd 9: *Yo, k1, k2tog, yo, k3, yo, ssk, k1, yo, k1; rep from * around—48 sts.
Rnd 11: *Yo, k3, yo, k1, p3tog, k1, yo, k3, yo, k1; rep from * around—56 sts.
Rnd 13: *Yo, k2, k2tog, yo, k5, yo, ssk, k2, yo, k1; rep from * around—64 sts.
Rnd 15: *Yo, k4, yo, k2, p3tog, k2, yo, k4, yo, k1; rep from * around—72 sts.
Rnd 17: *Yo, k3, k2tog, yo, k7, yo, ssk, k3, yo, k1; rep from * around—80 sts.
Rnd 19: *Yo, k5, yo, k3, p3tog, k3, yo, k5, yo, k1; rep from * around—88 sts.
Rnd 21: *Yo, k4, k2tog, yo, k9, yo, ssk, k4, yo, k1; rep from * around—96 sts.
Rnd 23: *Yo, k6, yo, k4, p3tog, k4, yo, k6, yo, k1; rep from * around—104 sts.
Rnd 25: *Yo, k5, k2tog, yo, k11, yo, ssk, k5, yo, k1; rep from * around—112 sts.
Rnd 27: *Yo, k7, yo, k5, p3tog, k5, yo, k7, yo, k1; rep from * around—120 sts.
Rnd 29: *Yo, k6, k2tog, yo, k1, yo, ssk, k7, k2tog, yo, k1, yo, ssk, k6, yo, k1; rep from * around—128 sts.
Rnd 31: *Yo, k8, yo, p3tog, yo, k9, yo, p3tog, yo, k8, yo, k1; rep from * around—136 sts.
Rnd 33: *Yo, k7, k2tog, yo, k3, yo, ssk, k5, k2tog, yo, k3, yo, ssk, k7, yo, k1; rep from * around—114 sts.
Rnd 35: *Yo, k9, yo, k1, p3tog, k1, yo, k7, yo, k1, p3tog, k1, yo, k9, yo, k1; rep from * around—152 sts.
Rnd 37: *Yo, k8, k2tog, yo, k5, yo, ssk, k3, k2tog, yo, k5, yo, ssk, k8, yo, k1; rep from * around—160 sts.
Rnd 39: *Yo, k10, yo, k2, p3tog, k2, yo, k5, yo, k2, p3tog, k2, yo, k10, yo, k1; rep from * around—168 sts.
Rnd 41: *Yo, k9, k2tog, yo, k7, yo, ssk, k1, k2tog, yo, k7, yo, ssk, k9, yo, k1; rep from * around—176 sts.
Rnd 43: *Yo, k11, yo, k3, p3tog, k3, yo, k3, yo, k3, p3tog, k3, yo, k11, yo, k1; rep from * around—184 sts.
Rnd 45: *Yo, k10, k2tog, yo, k9, yo, sl1, k2tog, psso, yo, k9, yo, ssk, k10, yo, k1; rep from * around—192 sts.
Rnd 47: *Yo, k10, k2tog, yo, k4, p3tog, k4, yo [k1, yo, k1] into next st, yo, k4, p3tog, k4, yo, ssk, k10, yo, k1; rep from * around—200 sts.
Rnd 49: *Yo, k10, k2tog, yo, k11, yo, sl1, k2tog, psso, yo, k11, yo, ssk, k10, yo, k1; rep from * around—208 sts.
Rnd 51: *Yo, k12, yo, k5, p3tog, k5, yo, k1, yo, k5, p3tog, k5, yo, k12, yo, k1; rep from * around—216 sts.
Rnd 53: *Yo, k11, k2tog, yo, ssk, k9, k2tog, yo [k1, yo, k1] into next st, yo, ssk, k9, k2tog, yo, ssk, k11, yo, k1; rep from * around—224 sts.
Rnd 55: *Yo, k11, k2tog, yo, k1, yo, ssk, k7, k2tog, yo, k2tog, yo, k1, yo, k2tog, yo, ssk, k7, k2tog, yo, k1, yo, ssk, k11, yo, k1; rep from * around—232 sts.

Rnd 57: *Yo, k9 [k2tog] 2 times, yo, k1 [k1, yo, k1] into next st, k1, yo, ssk, k5, k2tog, yo, k1, ssk, k1, k2tog, k1, yo, ssk, k5, k2tog, yo, k1 [k1, yo, k1] into next st, k1, yo [ssk] 2 times, k9, yo, k1; rep from * around—240 sts.

Rnd 59: *Yo, k10, k2tog, yo, k2tog, yo, k3, yo, k2tog, yo [ssk, k3, k2tog, yo, k2tog, yo, k3, yo, ssk, yo] 2 times, ssk, k10, yo, k1; rep from * around—248 sts.

Rnd 61: *Yo, k8 [k2tog] 2 times [yo, k2tog] 2 times, yo, k1 [yo, k2tog] 2 times, yo, ssk, k1, k2tog, yo, k2tog, yo, k2, yo, k1, yo, k2, yo, k2tog, yo, ssk, k1, k2tog [yo, k2tog] 2 times, yo, k1 [yo, k2tog] 2 times, yo [ssk] 2 times, k8, yo, k1; rep from * around—256 sts.

Rnd 63: *Yo, k9, k2tog, yo [k2tog, yo] 2 times, k3 [yo, k2tog] 2 times, yo, sl1, k2tog, psso, yo [k2tog, yo] 3 times, k1 [yo, k2tog] 3 times, yo, sl1, k2tog, psso, yo [k2tog, yo] 2 times, k3 [yo, k2tog] 2 times, yo, ssk, k9, yo, k1; rep from * around—264 sts.

Rnd 65: *Yo, k7 [k2tog] 2 times, yo [k2tog, yo] 3 times, k1 [yo, ssk] 3 times, yo, k1, yo [k2tog, yo] 3 times, sl1, k2tog, psso [yo, ssk] 3 times, yo, k1, yo [k2tog, yo] 3 times, k1 [yo, ssk] 3 times, yo [ssk] 2 times, k7, yo, k1; rep from * around—272 sts.

Rnd 67: *Yo, k8, k2tog, yo [k2tog, yo] 3 times, k3 [yo, ssk] 3 times, k1 [k2tog, yo] 3 times, k3 [yo, ssk] 3 times, k1 [k2tog, yo] 3 times, k3 [yo, ssk] 3 times, yo, ssk, k8, yo, k1; rep from * around—280 sts.

Rnd 69: *Yo, k6 [k2tog] 2 times, yo [k2tog, yo] 4 times, k1 [yo, ssk] 3 times, k3 [k2tog, yo] 2 times, k1, yo, k3, yo, k1 [yo, ssk] 2 times, k3 [k2tog, yo] 3 times, k1 [yo, ssk] 4 times, yo [ssk] 2 times, k6, yo, k1; rep from * around—288 sts.

Rnd 71: *Yo, k7, k2tog, yo [k2tog, yo] 4 times, k3 [yo, ssk] 3 times, k1 [k2tog, yo] 4 times, k1 [yo, ssk] 4 times, k1 [k2tog, yo] 3 times, k3 [yo, ssk] 4 times, yo, ssk, k7, yo, k1; rep from * around—296 sts.

Rnd 73: *Yo, k5 [k2tog] 2 times, yo [k2tog, yo] 5 times, k1 [yo, ssk] 3 times, yo, k3, yo [k2tog, yo] 2 times, k2tog, k3, ssk [yo, ssk] 2 times, yo, k3, yo [k2tog, yo] 3 times, k1 [yo, ssk] 5 times, yo [ssk] 2 times, k5, yo, k1; rep from * around—304 sts.

Rnd 75: *Yo, k6, k2tog, yo [k2tog, yo] 5 times, k3 [yo, ssk] 3 times, yo, sl1, k2tog, psso, yo [k2tog, yo] 3 times, k3 [yo, ssk] 3 times, yo, k3tog, yo [k2tog, yo] 3 times, k3 [yo, ssk] 5 times, yo, ssk, k6, yo, k1; rep from * around—312 sts.

Rnd 77: *Yo, k4 [k2tog] 2 times, yo [k2tog, yo] 6 times, k1 [yo, ssk] 5 times, k1, yo [k2tog, yo] 3 times, k1 [yo, ssk] 3 times, k1, yo [k2tog, yo] 5 times, k1 [yo, ssk] 6 times, yo [ssk] 2 times, k4, yo, k1; rep from * around—320 sts.

Rnd 79: *Yo, k5, k2tog, yo [k2tog, yo] 6 times, k3 [yo, ssk] 5 times [k2tog, yo] 3 times, k3 [yo, ssk] 3 times [k2tog, yo] 5 times, k3 [yo, ssk] 6 times, yo, ssk, k5, yo, k1; rep from * around—328 sts.

Rnd 81: *Yo, k3 [k2tog] 2 times, yo [k2tog, yo] 7 times, k1 [yo, ssk] 6 times, yo [k2tog, yo] 3 times, k1 [yo, ssk] 3 times, yo [k2tog, yo] 6 times, k1 [yo, ssk] 7 times, yo [ssk] 2 times, k3, yo, k1; rep from * around—336 sts.

Rnd 83: *Yo, k4, k2tog, yo [k2tog, yo] 7 times, k3 [yo, ssk] 5 times, yo, sl1, k2tog, psso, yo [k2tog, yo] 2 times, k3 [yo, ssk] 2 times, yo, k3tog, yo [k2tog, yo] 5 times, k3 [yo, ssk] 7 times, yo, ssk, k4, yo, k1; rep from * around—344 sts.

Rnd 85: *Yo, k2 [k2tog] 2 times, yo [k2tog, yo] 8 times, k1 [yo, ssk] 7 times, k1, yo [k2tog, yo] 2 times, k1 [yo, ssk] 2 times, yo, k1 [k2tog, yo] 7 times, k1 [yo, ssk] 8 times, yo [ssk] 2 times, k2, yo, k1; rep from * around—352 sts.

Rnd 87: *Yo, k3, k2tog, yo [k2tog, yo] 8 times, k3 [yo, ssk] 7 times [k2tog, yo] 2 times, k3 [yo, ssk] 2 times [k2tog, yo] 7 times, k3 [yo, ssk] 8 times, yo, ssk, k3, yo, k1; rep from * around—360 sts.

Rnd 89: *Yo, k1 [k2tog] 2 times, yo [k2tog, yo] 9 times, k1 [yo, ssk] 8 times, yo [k2tog, yo] 2 times, k1 [yo, ssk] 2 times, yo [k2tog, yo] 8 times, k1 [yo, ssk] 9 times, yo [ssk] 2 times, k1, yo, k1; rep from * around—368 sts.

Rnd 91: *Yo, k2, k2tog, yo [k2tog, yo] 9 times, k3 [yo, ssk] 8 times, k1, k2tog, yo, k3, yo, ssk, k1 [k2tog, yo] 8 times, k3 [yo, ssk] 9 times, yo, ssk, k2, yo, k1; rep from * around—376 sts.

Rnd 93: *Yo [k2tog] 2 times, yo [k2tog, yo] 10 times, k1 [yo, ssk] 9 times, k1, yo, k2tog, yo, k1, yo, ssk, yo, k1 [k2tog, yo] 9 times, k1 [yo, ssk] 10 times, yo [ssk] 2 times, yo, k1; rep from * around—384 sts.

Rnd 95: *Yo, k1, k2tog, yo [k2tog, yo] 10 times, k3 [yo, ssk] 9 times, k2tog, yo, k3, yo, ssk [k2tog, yo] 9 times, k3 [yo, ssk] 10 times, yo, ssk, k1, yo, k1; rep from * around—392 sts.

Rnd 97: *Yo, k3tog, yo [k2tog, yo] 11 times, k1 [yo, ssk] 10 times, yo, k2tog, yo, k1, yo, ssk, yo [k2tog, yo] 10 times, k1 [yo, ssk] 11 times, yo, sl1, k2tog, psso, yo, k1; rep from * around—400 sts.

Rnd 99: *Yo [k2tog, yo] 12 times, k3 [yo, ssk] 10 times, k2tog, yo, k1, yo, ssk [k2tog, yo] 10 times, k3 [yo, ssk] 12 times, yo, k1, pm; rep from * around—408 sts.

Rnd 101: *Yo, knit to last st before marker, yo, k1; rep from * around—416 sts.

Rnd 102: *K1, purl to last 2 sts before marker, k2; rep from * around—416 sts.

Rnd 103: *Yo, k6, * k4, k2tog, yo, k1, yo, ssk, k4; rep from * to last 7 sts, k6, yo, k1; rep from * around—424 sts.

Rnd 105: *Yo, k2, yo, ssk, k3, * k3, k2tog, yo, k3, yo, ssk, k3; rep from * to last 8 sts, k3, k2tog, yo, k2, yo, k1; rep from * around—432 sts.

Rnd 107: *Yo, k2 [yo, ssk] 2 times, k2, * k2 [k2tog, yo] 2 times, k1 [yo, ssk] 2 times, k2; rep from * to last 9 sts, k2 [k2tog, yo] 2 times, k2, yo, k1; rep from * around—440 sts.

Rnd 109: *Yo, k4 [yo, ssk] 2 times, k2, * k1 [k2tog, yo] 2 times, k3 [yo, ssk] 2 times, k2; rep from * to last 10 sts, k1 [k2tog, yo] 2 times, k4, yo, k1; rep from * around—448 sts.

Rnd 111: *Yo, k1, k2tog, yo, k1 [yo, ssk] 3 times, * [k2tog, yo] 3 times, k1 [yo, ssk] 3 times; rep from * to last 11 sts [k2tog, yo] 3 times, k1, yo, ssk, k1, yo, k1; rep from * around—456 sts.

Rnd 113: Rep rnd 101—464 sts.

Rnd 114: Rep rnd 102—464 sts.

Rnd 115: *Yo, k1 [ssk, yo] 2 times, k1 [yo, k2tog] 3 times, * [ssk, yo] 3 times, k1 [yo, k2tog] 3 times; rep from * to last 13 sts [ssk, yo] 3 times, k1 [yo, k2tog] 2 times, k1, yo, k1; rep from * around—472 sts.

Rnd 117: *Yo, * k1 [ssk, yo] 2 times, k3 [yo, k2tog] 2 times, k1; rep from * to last st, yo, k1; rep from * around—480 sts.

Rnd 119: *Yo, k1, * k2 [ssk, yo] 2 times, k1 [yo, k2tog] 2 times, k2; rep from * to last 2 sts, k1, yo, k1; rep from * around—488 sts.

Rnd 121: *Yo, k2, * k3, ssk, yo, k3, yo, k2tog, k3; rep from * to last 3 sts, k2, yo, k1; rep from * around—496 sts.

Rnd 123: *Yo, k3, * k4, ssk, yo, k1, yo, k2tog, k4; rep from * to last 4 sts, k3, yo, k1; rep from * around—504 sts.

Rnd 125: Rep rnd 101—512 sts.

Rnd 126: Rep rnd 102—512 sts.

Rnd 127: Rep rnd 101—520 sts.

Rnd 128: Rep rnd 102—520 sts.

BO using twice-worked BO in purl, as follows: purl 2 sts, BO, * return st on right-hand needle to left-hand needle, p2tog, p1, BO; rep from * to end.

Finishing

Weave in ends. Block shawl to give it shape and open up the lace pattern.

Resources

Skill Levels for Knitting

1	◖□□□	**Beginner**	Projects for first-time knitters using basic knit and purl stitches. Minimal shaping.
2	◖■□□	**Easy**	Projects using basic stitches, repetitive stitch patterns, simple color changes, and simple shaping and finishing.
3	◖■■□	**Intermediate**	Projects with a variety of stitches, such as basic cables and lace, simple intarsia, double-pointed needles and knitting in the round needle techniques, mid-level shaping and finishing.
4	◖■■◗	**Experienced**	Projects using advanced techniques and stitches, such as short rows, Fair Isle, more intricate intarsia, cables, lace patterns, and numerous color changes.

Skill level, standard body measurements/sizing, and yarn weight information are courtesy of the Craft Yarn Council of America (http://www.craftyarncouncil.com).

Standard Body Measurements/Sizing

Most crochet and knitting pattern instructions will provide general sizing information, such as the chest or bust measurements of a completed garment. Many patterns also include detailed schematics or line drawings. These drawings show specific garment measurements (bust/chest, neckline, back, waist, sleeve length, etc.) in all the different pattern sizes. To ensure proper fit, always review all of the sizing information provided in a pattern before you begin.

Following are several sizing charts. These charts show Chest, Center Back Neck-to-Cuff, Back Waist Length, Cross Back, and Sleeve Length **actual body measurements** for babies, children, women, and men. These measurements are given in both inches and centimeters.

When sizing sweaters, the fit is based on actual chest/bust measurements, plus ease (additional inches or centimeters). The first chart entitled "Fit" recommends the amount of ease to add to body measurements if you prefer a close-fitting garment, an oversized garment, or something in-between.

The next charts provide average lengths for children's, women's, and men's garments.

Both the Fit and Length charts are simply guidelines. For individual body differences, changes can be made in body and sleeve lengths when appropriate. However, consideration must be given to the project pattern. Certain sizing changes may alter the appearance of a garment.

HOW TO MEASURE

1. Chest/Bust
Measure around the fullest part of the chest/bust. Do not draw the tape too tightly.

2. Center Back Neck–to–Cuff
With arm slightly bent, measure from back base of neck across shoulder around bend of elbow to wrist.

3. Back Waist Length
Measure from the most prominent bone at base of neck to the natural waistline.

4. Cross Back
Measure from shoulder to shoulder.

5. Sleeve Length
With arm slightly bent, measure from armpit to cuff.

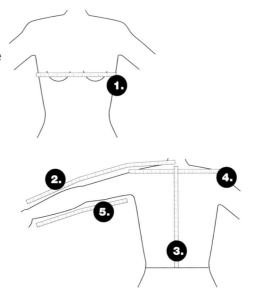

FIT

Very-close fitting: Actual chest/bust measurement or less
Close-fitting: 1–2"/2.5–5cm
Standard-fitting: 2–4"/5–10cm
Loose-fitting: 4–6"/10–15cm
Oversized: 6"/15cm or more

LENGTH FOR CHILDREN

Waist length: Actual body measurement
Hip length: 2"/5cm down from waist
Tunic length: 6"/15cm down from waist

LENGTH FOR WOMEN

Waist length: Actual body measurement
Hip length: 6"/15cm down from waist
Tunic length: 11"/28cm down from waist

LENGTH FOR MEN

Men's length usually varies only 1–2"/ 2.5–5cm from the actual "back hip length" measurement (*see chart*)

Baby's size	3 months	6 months	12 months	18 months	24 months
1. Chest (in.)	16	17	18	19	20
(cm.)	*40.5*	*43*	*45.5*	*48*	*50.5*
2. Center Back Neck-to-Cuff	10½	11½	12½	14	18
	26.5	*29*	*31.5*	*35.5*	*45.5*
3. Back Waist Length	6	7	7½	8	8½
	15.5	*17.5*	*19*	*20.5*	*21.5*
4. Cross Back (Shoulder to shoulder)	7¼	7¾	8¼	8½	8¾
	18.5	*19.5*	*21*	*21.5*	*22*
5. Sleeve Length to Underarm	6	6½	7½	8	8½
	15.5	*16.5*	*19*	*20.5*	*21.5*

Child's size	2	4	6	8	10
1. Chest (in.)	21	23	25	26½	28
(cm.)	*53*	*58.5*	*63.5*	*67*	*71*
2. Center Back Neck-to-Cuff	18	19½	20½	22	24
	45.5	*49.5*	*52*	*56*	*61*
3. Back Waist Length	8½	9½	10½	12½	14
	21.5	*24*	*26.5*	*31.5*	*35.5*
4. Cross Back (Shoulder to shoulder)	9¼	9¾	10¼	10¾	11¼
	23.5	*25*	*26*	*27*	*28.5*
5. Sleeve Length to Underarm	8½	10½	11½	12½	13½
	21.5	*26.5*	*29*	*31.5*	*34.5*

Standard Body Measurements/Sizing
(continued)

Child's (cont.)	12	14	16
1. Chest (in.)	30	31½	32½
(cm.)	76	80	82.5
2. Center Back Neck-to-Cuff	26	27	28
	66	68.5	71
3. Back Waist Length	15	15½	16
	38	39.5	40.5
4. Cross Back (Shoulder to Shoulder)	12	12¼	13
	30.5	31	33
5. Sleeve Length to Underarm	15	16	16½
	38	40.5	42

Woman's size	X-Small	Small	Medium	Large
1. Bust (in.)	28–30	32–34	36–38	40–42
(cm.)	71–76	81–86	91.5–96.5	101.5–106.5
2. Center Back Neck-to-Cuff	27–27½	28–28½	29–29½	30–30½
	68.5–70	71–72.5	73.5–75	76–77.5
3. Back Waist Length	16½	17	17¼	17½
	42	43	43.5	44.5
4. Cross Back (Shoulder to Shoulder)	14–14½	14½–15	16–16½	17–17½
	35.5–37	37–38	40.5–42	43–44.5
5. Sleeve Length to Underarm	16½	17	17	17½
	42	43	43	44.5

Woman's (cont.)	1X	2X	3X	4X	5X
1. Bust (in.)	44–46	48–50	52–54	56–58	60–62
(cm.)	111.5–117	122–127	132–137	142–147	152–158
2. Center Back Neck-to-Cuff	31–31½	31½–32	32½–33	32½–33	33–33½
	78.5–80	80–81.5	82.5–84	82.5–84	84–85
3. Back Waist Length	17¾	18	18	18½	18½
	45	45.5	45.5	47	47
4. Cross Back (Shoulder to Shoulder)	17½	18	18	18½	18½
	44.5	45.5	45.5	47	47
5. Sleeve Length to Underarm	17½	18	18	18½	18½
	44.5	45.5	45.5	47	47

Man's Size	Small	Medium	Large	X-Large	XX-Large
1. Chest (in.)	34–36	38–40	42–44	46–48	50–52
(cm.)	*86–91.5*	*96.5–101.5*	*106.5–111.5*	*116.5–122*	*127–132*
2. Center Back Neck-to-Cuff	32–32½	33–33½	34–34½	35–35½	36–36½
	81–82.5	*83.5–85*	*86.5–87.5*	*89–90*	*91.5–92.5*
3. Back Hip Length	25–25½	26½–26¾	27–27¼	27½–27¾	28–28½
	63.5–64.5	*67.5–68*	*68.5–69*	*69.5–70.5*	*71–72.5*
4. Cross Back (Shoulder to Shoulder)	15½–16	16½–17	17½–18	18–18½	18½–19
	39.5–40.5	*42–43*	*44.5–45.5*	*45.5–47*	*47–48*
5. Sleeve Length to Underarm	18	18½	19½	20	20½
	45.5	*47*	*49.5*	*50.5*	*52*

Head Circumference Chart

	Infant/Child				Adult	
	Premie	**Baby**	**Toddler**	**Child**	**Woman**	**Man**
6. Circumference						
(in.)	12	14	16	18	20	22
(cm.)	*30.5*	*35.5*	*40.5*	*45.5*	*50.5*	*56*

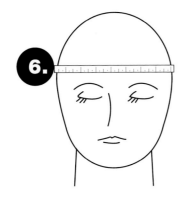

For an accurate head measure, place a tape measure across the forehead and measure around the full circumference of the head. Keep the tape snug for accurate results.

STANDARDS & GUIDELINES FOR CROCHET AND KNITTING

Standard Yarn Weight System

Categories of yarn, gauge ranges, and recommended needle and hook sizes

Yarn Weight Symbol & Category Names	0 Lace	1 Super Fine	2 Fine	3 Light	4 Medium	5 Bulky	6 Super Bulky
Type of Yarns in Category	Fingering 10 count crochet thread	Sock, Fingering, Baby	Sport, Baby	DK, Light Worsted	Worsted, Afghan, Aran	Chunky, Craft, Rug	Bulky, Roving
Knit Gauge Range* in Stockinette Stitch to 4 inches	33–40** sts	27–32 sts	23–26 sts	21–24 sts	16–20 sts	12–15 sts	6–11 sts
Recommended Needle in Metric Size Range	1.5–2.25 mm	2.25–3.25 mm	3.25–3.75 mm	3.75–4.5 mm	4.5–5.5 mm	5.5–8 mm	8 mm and larger
Recommended Needle U.S. Size Range	000 to 1	1 to 3	3 to 5	5 to 7	7 to 9	9 to 11	11 and larger
Crochet Gauge* Ranges in Single Crochet to 4 inch	32-42 double crochets**	21–32 sts	16–20 sts	12–17 sts	11–14 sts	8–11 sts	5–9 sts
Recommended Hook in Metric Size Range	Steel*** 1.6–1.4mm Regular hook 2.25 mm	2.25–3.5 mm	3.5–4.5 mm	4.5–5.5 mm	5.5–6.5 mm	6.5–9 mm	9 mm and larger
Recommended Hook U.S. Size Range	Steel*** 6, 7, 8 Regular hook B–1	B–1 to E–4	E–4 to 7	7 to I–9	I–9 to K–10½	K–10½ to M–13	M–13 and larger

* GUIDELINES ONLY: The above reflect the most commonly used gauges and needle or hook sizes for specific yarn categories.

** Lace weight yarns are usually knitted or crocheted on larger needles and hooks to create lacy, openwork patterns. Accordingly, a gauge range is difficult to determine. Always follow the gauge stated in your pattern.

*** Steel crochet hooks are sized differently from regular hooks--the higher the number, the smaller the hook, which is the reverse of regular hook sizing.

This Standards & Guidelines booklet and downloadable symbol artwork are available at: **YarnStandards.com**

Knitting Abbreviations

beg	beginning
bl	back loop(s)
BO	bind off
CC	contrasting color
cm	centimeter(s)
CO	cast on
cont	continue
dec	decrease/decreasing
fl	front loop(s)
g	gram(s)
inc	increase/increasing
k	knit
k2tog	knit 2 stitches together
kwise	knitwise
lp(s)	loop(s)
m	meter(s)
M1	make one
MC	main color
mm	millimeter(s)
oz	ounce(s)
p	purl
patt	pattern
pm	place marker
p2tog	purl 2 stitches together
prev	previous
psso	pass slipped stitch over
p2sso	pass 2 slipped stitches over
pwise	purlwise

rem	remaining
rep	repeat
rev St st	reverse stockinette stitch
rnd(s)	round(s)
RS	right side
sk	skip
skp	slip, knit, pass
sk2p	slip 1, k2tog, pass slipped stitch over
sl	slip
sl1k	slip 1 knitwise
sl1p	slip 1 purlwise
spp	slip, purl, pass
ssk	slip, slip, knit
st(s)	stitch(es)
St st	stockinette stitch
tbl	through the back loop(s)
tog	together
WS	wrong side
wyib	with yarn in back
wyif	with yarn in front
yd	yard(s)
yo	yarn over
[ ]	work instructions within brackets as many times as directed
( )	work instructions within brackets in the place directed
*	repeat instructions following the asterisk as directed
"	inch(es)

Standard Stitch Chart Symbols

☐	K on RS, p on WS	ℚ	K1 tbl on RS, p1 tbl on WS
▨	P on RS, k on WS	ℚ	P1 tbl on RS, k1 tbl on WS
—	P on RS, k on WS on a color chart	●	Bobble
O	Yarn over (yo)	▨	Sts do not exist in these areas of chart (70% shade)
/	K2tog on RS, p2tog on WS	M	Make 1 (M1) knitwise on RS, M1 purlwise on WS
/	p2tog on RS, K2tog on WS	M	Make 1 (M1) purlwise on RS, M1 knitwise on WS
\	SSK on RS, SSP on WS	Ⅴ	Inc 1-to-3
\	SSP on RS, SSK on WS	Ⅴ⁴	Inc 1-to-4
Ⴌ	Right-slanting inc	Ⅴ⁵	Inc 1-to-5
Ⴘ	Left-slanting inc	∕₄	Dec 4-to-1 (right-slanting)
V	Sl 1 purlwise with yarn at WS of work	↘₄	Dec 4-to-1 (left-slanting)
Ⴥ	Sl 1 purlwise with yarn at RS of work	Λ₄	Dec 4-to-1 (vertical)
∕₃	K3tog on RS, p3tog on WS	Λ₅	Dec 5-to-1
₃\	SK2P, SSSK on RS, SSSP on WS	ℛ	K1, wrapping yarn twice around needle
Λ	S2KP2 on RS, S2PP2 on WS	⌒	Bind off

Visual Index of Projects

Gillian Cowl
page 114

Bayside Scarf
page 120

Universal Kite Shawlette
page 128

Heart's Content Scarf
page 116

McDaisy Tablet or Laptop Sleeve
page 122

Comfort in Diamonds Throw
page 132

Tionesta Lake Throw
page 118

Adirondack Mittens
page 125

Sugar Run Skirt
page 135

Twin Lakes Cover-Up and Hat
page 138

Teddy Bear Sweater
page 153

Bamboo Forest Sweater
page 168

Beaver Meadows Felted Purse
page 142

Biscayne Bay Shell
page 156

Wintry Mix Hat
page 171

Tracy Ridge Hat
page 146

Roxbury Park Cardigan
page 160

Lantz Corners Shawl
page 174

Big Rock Socks
page 150

Bottom-Up Cardigan
page 164